Monte Perdido. NE face and Pineta lake (Lac Glacé) from the Brèche de Tuquerouye.

Pyrenees West

LARRAU TO GAVARNIE CIRQUE

A GUIDE TO THE MOUNTAINS FOR WALKERS AND CLIMBERS

Arthur Battagel

GASTONS - WEST COL

PYRENEES WEST

Second Edition 1988

Gastons West Col Publications

Goring   Reading   Berks. RG8 9AA

SBN   906227 33 X

Companion volumes:
Pyrenees Central (formerly East)
Pyrenees East (formerly Andorra Cerdagne)
Pyrenees High Level Route

Printed in England by
Swindon Press   Swindon   Wilts.

Contents

Illustrations

Photos by : J.M. Sala Albareda, Bernard Clos, Juan Cortázar, Angel López.

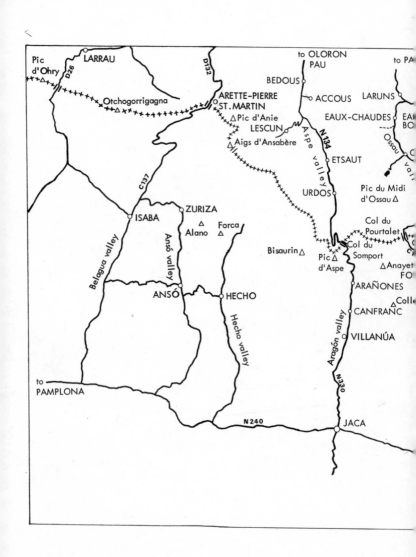

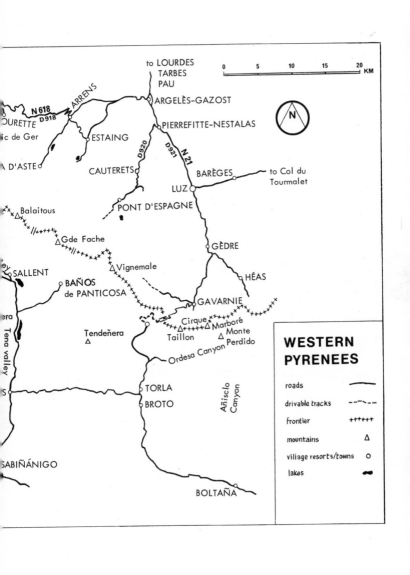

to LOURDES
TARBES
PAU

0 5 10 15 20 KM

N

ARRENS

N 618

OURETTE
D 918

ic de Ger

ESTAING

ARGELÈS-GAZOST

PIERREFITTE-NESTALAS

A D'ASTE

CAUTERETS

D 920

D 921

N 21

BARÈGES

to Col du
Tourmalet

LUZ

PONT D'ESPAGNE

Balaitous

Gde Fache

Vignemale

GÈDRE

HÉAS

ley
SALLENT

BAÑOS
de PANTICOSA

GAVARNIE

Cirque

Marboré

Taillon

Monte
Perdido

era

Tena valley

Tendeñera

Ordesa Canyon

TORLA

BROTO

Añisclo
Canyon

S

SABIÑÁNIGO

BOLTAÑA

**WESTERN
PYRENEES**

roads ———

drivable tracks - - -

frontier +++++

mountains △

village resorts/towns ○

lakes �

ABBREVIATIONS

Br.	Brèche (gap)
CAF	French Alpine Club
EA	Editorial Alpina (maps)
FEM	Spanish Mountain Federation
Fr.	France, French
G	IGN Green tourist map series
Gde.	Grande
GR	Long distance trail (n. 10)
h.	hour(s)
HRP	Pyrenees High Level Route trail (English code: HP)
IGC	Spanish national mapping agency (several variables)
IGN	French national mapping agency
km.	kilometres
L	left (direction)
m.	metre(s)
m.	against map scale = 1,000, eg. 25m. = 1/25,000 50m. = 1/50,000 etc.
min.	minutes
n.	map sheet number
PNP	Pyrenees (French) National Park
pt.	point, map spot height
R	right (direction)
RN	Route nationale (main road)
RP	Randonnées Pyrénéennes Association
Sp.	Spain, Spanish
TCF	French Touring Club
V	IGN Violet tourist map series
var.	variation, variant

compass directions: N, S, E, W, and intermediate directions, eg. NW, SE, etc.

Introduction

A map of Europe usually shows the Pyrenees as no more than a single chain of mountains that forms a natural frontier between France and Spain running from the Atlantic to the Mediterranean for a distance of about 400 km. A larger scale map will reveal that this is a simplification and that there is no continuous range but 2 main ones which generally, but with notable exceptions, form the watershed and the frontier. In France the foothills rise abruptly from the plain, but in Spain the picture is different. It is not always easy to define the S limit of the Pyrenees because the whole area between them and the great Ebro valley is mountainous.

The main Western range runs eastwards from the Atlantic to end at a gap where the Garonne river flows from Spain into France. The Eastern range runs from this gap to the Mediterranean, but starts some way to the N of the end of the Western range.

There are, however, important massifs lying both to the N and to the S of the frontier. To the N is the so-called Eaux-Bonnes limestone massif and also the Néouvielle group. S of the frontier, entirely in Spain, are the 3 highest massifs of the Pyrenees – Perdido, Posets and Maladeta. Also in Spain is a fragmented limestone range of some importance; it lies at an angle to the main frontier range, extending ESE from the Bisaurin (close to the frontier just W of the Aragon valley) to the Turbón (S of Benasque, in the Central Pyrenees). Its main summits are Collarada, Tendeñera and Cotiella; this last (2912 m.) is the highest in the range.

From the Atlantic, where they are no more than hills, the Pyrenees rise in height very gradually eastwards through the wooded Basque country for some 70 km. before true mountains are reached with the Pic d'Orhy in the Larrau-Haute Soule district. To the S of that area in Spain are a number of summits exceeding 2000 m. in height.

On the frontier, towards the border between the Departments of the Pyrénées Atlantiques and the Hautes Pyrénées, heights rise to almost 3000 m. In this area stands the monumental Pic du Midi d'Ossau, a goal for the ardent rock climber. Then follows a series of frontier peaks all above 3000 m., separated by high passes and with a spur pushed out SE into Spain to form the Monte Perdido group a little to the SE of Gavarnie.

While the Pyrenees are naturally divided into western and eastern sections by the Garonne gap, this guide covers an area only as far E as Monte Perdido and the Añisclo canyon. To complete the general outline it may be mentioned that from the Troumouse group, E of Gavarnie, the frontier for the next 20 km. falls well below the 3000m. mark until it reaches the Pic de Batoua, whence it continues to rise before sinking again to the Garonne gap. To the S of this stretch of high frontier lies the huge Posets massif, with the Pyrenees' second highest summit; then further E is the higher Maladeta massif, a long ridge generally above 3200m. that includes the Pico de Aneto, the highest point in Europe outside the Alps, with the unexpected exception of the Mulhacen and other summits in the Sierra Nevada of southern Spain. To the E of the Maladeta massif, and also in Spain, is the beautiful lake-studded area known as the Encantados.

E of the Garonne gap the general level of the range is lower, with only 3 peaks topping the 3000m. level, but with several summits falling just short of it.

SCOPE OF GUIDE

In dealing with so extensive an area it is clearly not possible to cover even every simple ascent, let along every rock climb. Indeed this is not the purpose of the guide. It is merely hoped to give a reasonably balanced picture of the greater part of the area, describing the main massifs and peaks, the huts, routes to them and some of the more interesting scrambles from them. While reference will be made to some of the more important rock climbs, those wishing to attempt them should consult French and Spanish climbing guides - see note at back of book.

NATIONAL PARKS

The Pyrenees National Park (PNP), in France, was inaugurated in 1967. It consists of an area of irregular depth bounded on the S by the frontier and stretching from a little to the E of the Pic d'Anie in the Lescun group to beyond Gavarnie in the E. A large part of the French area covered in this guide is thus within the area of the Park.

The PNP authority has been very active, building huts, improving some of the more popular paths and marking them by red and white horizontal bands, erecting signposts - many of which are destroyed each winter by the elements - and providing refuse baskets. It has opened a handsome Reception Centre at Plaa d'Aste where the road running up the Val d' Azun from Arrens ends and where general information is gladly given.

While one of the main objects of the Park, the preservation of natural beauty, can only be applauded, another is the throwing open of the area to a much wider public, many of which lack even basic knowledge of mountain-craft; this policy is less easy to comprehend. An increase in visitors brings with it an increase in control - the last thing mountain lovers want. Improvement of some paths to high club huts has led many without experience into areas where a sudden change of weather can easily place them in real danger. Aware of the influx of the uninitiated, the PNP has found it necessary to set up rather too many rustic notice boards telling us authoritatively what not to do in mountains. However, this is mild criticism compared with observations that can be made about appalling trends in French alpine national parks.

The Ordesa National Park in Spain, of older date than the PNP, comprises the Ordesa valley and an area on both sides of it. Northwards it extends to the frontier and thus adjoins the eastern part of the PNP above Gavarnie. It is surrounded, except to the N, by a large game reserve. In this Park preservation of the astonishing beauty it contains has taken precedence over 'improvements', but here too road building and upgrading amenities threatens to make considerable advances in the near future.

WEATHER

The Pyrenees lie in a latitude almost as far S as Rome, a point easily forgotten in the lush green valleys of France. A short journey into the valleys of Spain will soon convince that these are indeed southern mountains. Weather during the months from mid June to early September can usually be relied upon to be good. You will be unlucky if more than 2 or 3 days of rain are met within a fortnights' vacation. Obviously there can be exceptions, and snowfall down to 2000m. has been seen in late July.

On the French side thick clouds tend to form in the valleys during the afternoon and rise very rapidly to the peaks, bringing visibility down to a few m. Occasionally they will be dispelled late in the evening but more often they will persist until sunrise next morning. It is therefore prudent to make a very early start on high expeditions so that you can be back at the hut or down in the valley by 2 or 3 o'clock at the latest. The Spanish valleys are not usually subject to this snag.

Temperatures during the summer months are not as high as the latitude might suggest. Starting points in the valleys are generally 1300m. to 1500m. but, even so, the pack-laden trudge up to the hut, if not taken in the early morning, can be hotter than is comfortable, especially on the Spanish side.

MAIN ROCK CLIMBING CENTRES

All but a few summits in the area covered by this volume can be reached without rock climbing proper, but this should not be taken to mean that these same peaks do not offer good technical ascents for the rock climber. The main climbing areas, taken from W to E, are:

a) Aigs. d'Ansabère, which have a tragic history - related anon.
b) Pic d'Ossau. A great variety of routes in all grades of difficulty on this granite mountain.
c) Balaitous. Graded climbs on some of the ridges.
d) Vignemale N face.
e) Cirque de Gavarnie. On its various walls.
f) Cilindro. Some of its faces, etc.
g) Tozal del Mallo and Punta Galliñero in the Ordesa valley.
h) Alano massif N face, in Spain, and other faces of the Southern Limestone Range in Spain.

GEOLOGY

The Pyrenees are a geological patchwork of great complexity and no attempt is made to explain the detail. In general terms the regions of Pierre St. Martin, Lescun and the Aspe group are limestone. So is the fragmented southern range, entirely in Spain. Between Pierre St. Martin and the Lescun group is a fantastic 'Karst' area. The Pic d'Ossau is purplish-brown granite. The Balaitous is also granite but of a rust colour. The Eaux-Bonnes group is limestone, characterised by great slabs which appear disquietingly smooth until approached; then they will be found to have the texture of coarse sandpaper to which vibram soles adhere reassuringly. From Vignemale to the Monte Perdido group inclusive, limestone again but of a different quality from either that of Lescun or Eaux-Bonnes. The cliffs of the Ordesa and Añisclo canyons in Spain, also limestone, are as highly coloured as the Grand Canyon in the USA.

CAVING

The presence of several limestone formations will rightly suggest opportunities for underground exploration. The most western area in this guide contains the world-famous caves and underground galleries and rivers in the neighbourhood of Pierre St. Martin. Exploration of these caves commenced seriously in the early 1950s and one system reached to a depth of 1342m. The EA map-guide booklet no.201 lists all these caves, some of which are shown on the map. The Spanish word for cave is 'sima', the French 'gouffre'.

Apart from this district, there is that of Causiat in the Aspe mountains, about 3km. W of the Col du Somport. The high plateau between the Cirque de Gavarnie and the Ordesa valley also holds caves, notably the Grotte Casteret.

ROAD ACCESS

In recent years there has been considerable re-classification and re-numbering of roads in France. If older maps of any scale are used there may be some confusion with roadsigns now seen. Even some current maps use a mixture of old and new road numbers, and others show both old and new. Michelin maps may be more reliable in this motoring context than IGN.

Most visitors from Britain will approach the Western and West Central Pyrenees from the N. The 2 main towns to make for are Pau and Tarbes. From either good roads continue S to penetrate all valleys described in this guide. At the Larrau, Pierre St. Martin, Somport, Pourtalet and Gavarnie cols, roads enter Spain and give access to previously more remote Spanish massifs in this sector of the range. All are toll free except for the Spanish side of the Port de Gavarnie.

PARKING FACILITIES

There are a few large carparks, viz at Pont d'Espagne, Gavarnie and Astún. Locked cars can usually be left in safety for several days at any spot on the roadside in both France and Spain. At most places where paths leave a road for the huts a small group of cars will be found in a convenient layby. It is prudent to conceal from view articles of value and items such as transistors, the use of which, incidentally, is strictly prohibited in all club huts.

RAIL ACCESS

In France, as in Britain, many uneconomic branch lines have been closed. The line from Pau to Jaca, roughly following the N.134 road, was cut by a landslide 20 years ago and to date remains closed. From Pau trains run to Oloron-Ste. Marie where French railways (SNCF) offer a linking bus service over the Somport col to Arañones (Canfranc) station. These buses stop at all abandoned stations and in Urdos village. From Canfranc a rail service runs down to Jaca, Sabiñánigo and points S. The line from Pau to Laruns is now closed, also the one from Lourdes to Pierrefitte-Nestalas in the Gave de Pau valley.

PUBLIC TRANSPORT

A railway-bus service runs from Buzy (the old rail junction from which the line formerly ran up to Laruns) to Laruns, Eaux-Bonnes and Gourette. A similar service runs from Lourdes up the valley of the Gave de Pau to Pierrefitte-Nestalas, Cauterets, Luz, Barèges (on the Luz to Col du Tourmalet road) and Gavarnie. There is no bus service up the Ossau valley beyond Laruns.

ACCOMMODATION

Larrau - Haute Soule

Small hotel in Larrau. Arette-Pierre St.Martin; small hotel, inn; main hotel burnt down but is due to be rebuilt.

Aspe valley

Bedous - several small and fairly cheap hotels. Lescun - Hôtel du Pic d'Anie, 1 star, fairly comfortable but not cheap. Etsaut - Hôtel des Pyrénées, frequently booked up, good food at reasonable prices; also Hôtel des Voyageurs, 2 star. Urdos - Hôtel des Voyageurs, 1 star, good but not cheap; several smaller establishments. Hôtel Le Somport, 2 star; Hôtel Le Pas d'Aspe, 1 star.

Ossau valley

Eaux-Chaudes, 2 or 3 smallish hotels. Gabas - Hôtel des Pyrénées is closed to public; 2 smaller hotels. Col du Pourtalet - inn with 2 or 3 simple rooms only; dormitory in loft, plain but good restaurant, kind and good-natured service.

Laruns - Argelès road

Eaux-Bonnes, several hotels. Gourette - skiing centre; several hotels of varying prices open in summer. Arrens - small but pleasant hotel. Lac d'Estaing, Vallée de Bun; small hotel.

Gave de Pau valley

Southwards from Lourdes there is a string of villages, all with hotels, but not likely to be of interest, being too far from mountain centres. Cauterets - a large variety at all prices. Pont d'Espagne has a small fairly comfortable hotel but not cheap. Gèdre has 3 hotels.
Gavarnie: Hôtel des Voyageurs, an historic hotel, over 200 years in the same family, good but not cheap. This famous establishment has been frequented by all the great names in Pyrenean exploration. Other smaller hotels. Rooms can be obtained at various houses in the village. Hotel access by path only, 4km. S of village.

Belagua, Ansó-Hecho valleys

Isaba; several hotels. Hecho; 2 hotels. Ansó; 2 small hotels.

Aragón valley

Candanchu: ski resort, many hotels, some open in summer. Canfranc; several hotels. Villanúa; several hotels. Astún; ski resort, some hotels open in summer.

Gállego valley

Formigal: ski resort, several hotels open in summer. Sallent; small hotel. Balneario de Panticosa: large but reasonably priced hotels.

Ara and Ordesa valleys

Torla; several small hotels, fairly cheap; a large new hotel 1.5 km. N of village on road to Ordesa valley. Ordesa: state hotel (Parador) at entrance to valley; good but expensive; sometimes found closed.

HUTS

France

Handbooks are published in France and Spain purporting to list all huts in the Pyrenees, complete with basic access details and facilities/amenities provided. This kind of information tends to go out of date quickly. The numerous huts of the French Alpine Club (CAF) all have hut-keepers unless otherwise stated. The reduced price for CAF members and members of reciprocating alpine clubs of other countries rises annually, like most other services, and in 1987 was about £4 for dormitory accommodation. Non members pay double. Huts with keepers provide a meals service (not cheap), and prices are the same for every one. Self-catering is usually possible.

The PNP Authority has built a number of pleasant huts designed and sited for the walker rather than the climber. Charges are similar to CAF huts; also other services. The RP Association has opened a number of Gîtes d'Étapes - well appointed but simple huts for walkers. These have no hut-keepers and do not provide food; a hut-minder, to whom payment is made, lives nearby. RP huts provide bunks, blankets, toilet facilities, stoves and cooking utensils with accommodation for about 15 persons. Dates of opening given below are subject to alteration if heavy snow persists.

Larrau - Haute Soule

Logibar Gîte d'Étape   380m. RP, 15 places, D.26, 2½ km. E of Larrau.

Senta hut   640m.
Private gîte. In Senta hamlet at D.113 roadhead. 15 places, open
all year.

Relais de la Pierre St.Martin   1650m.
In Arette-Pierre St.Martin ski resort, an inn rather than a hut with 12
places, full services, open 10 June-30October, and 1 December-1 May.
Frequently full, check in advance by ringing 39.19.01 (add 59 for long
distance). There are 2 other huts in this neighbourhood.

Lescun Area

Labérouat (Labourat) hut   1442m.
Can now be reached by road from Lescun, 40 places, open all year
round except September-December. Not recommended.

Aspe Valley

Lac d'Arlet hut   1988m.
PNP. 36 places. Situated just N of the frontier, SW of Urdos. Reached
from Etsaut by a 4-5 h. walk. Open 1 July-30 September.

Larry hut   1724m.
PNP. 10 places, no hut-keeper, no food; bunks and mattresses. Found
SE of Urdos, and reached from there by a $2\frac{1}{2}$-3 h. walk.

Ossau Valley

Gabas hut   1035m.
CAF. 55 places. A valley hut situated on the hair-pin bend to the S
of Gabas village. All services, open throughout the year.

Pombie hut   2032m.
CAF. 48 places, self-catering, situated directly beneath the Pombie
wall of the Pic du Midi. Very good, clean and well-run, often crowded.
In additional to normal accommodation, a large tent with spring mattresses and blankets for 16 persons is put up when necessary. Open 30 June-
15 September. Routes to this hut are described in the Pic d'Ossau part.

Lac d'Ayous hut   1960m
PNP. 30 places. Reached by a well marked and signposted path from
Bious Artigues lake and roadhead in a walk of 5-6km. to the SW on the
high plateau between the Ossau and Aspe valleys. Open from 15 June
to 30 September.

Arrémoulit hut   2304m.
CAF. 30 places, plus tent for 16 when necessary. Open 30 June to
15 October. On the edge of the small Arrémoulit lake beneath the W
face of Pic Palas. Starting point for the Balaitous, Palas and Arriel.
For access to hut, see under Balaitous.

Gourette hut   1350m.
CAF. Not in the Ossau valley but in Gourette on the Laruns-Col d'
Aubisque road. Built primarily for winter use, open during summer at
weekends, school holidays and on request. Booking for large parties
with CAF Section Sud-Ouest, 17 Cours Xavier-Arnozan, 33000
Bordeaux.

Azun Valley

Larribet hut   2070m.
CAF. 45 places, but being enlarged to cope with 75. Open 1 June-
30 September. The hut stands to the N of the Balaitous; see latter
for access.

Balaitous (Ledormeur) hut   1917m.
CAF. An old, small hut with no keeper, poor facilities. On the
western slopes of the upper Azun valley to the E of the Balaitous, qv
for access.

Migouélou hut   2278m.
PNP. 40 places. Open 1 July-15 September. Reached by a path
starting from roadhead at Plaa d'Aste in the Azun valley; a good 3 h.
trek to the W in fine walking country.

Cauterets Area

Raymond Ritter hut   1985m.
PNP. Previously called Ilhéou hut. 32 places, open 15 June to 30
September. W of Cauterets in the Saulx valley. From Courbet road-
head, $1\frac{1}{2}$ h. on foot.

Wallon hut   1865m.
CAF. This old hut stands on an idyllic site in the upper Marcadau valley. 80 places, open 10 June-30 September. Recently taken over
from the TCF and much improved. Restaurant service, often crowded
due to short, easy walk S from Pont d'Espagne roadhead.

Oulétes de Gaube hut   2151m.
CAF. Below the N face of the Vignemale. 80 places, self-catering
facilities, open 1 June-30 September. A splendid hut in a magnificent
setting, reached by a good, easy path from Pont d'Espagne, through the
Gaube valley. See under Vignemale.

Estom hut   1804m.
Small inn at the Estom lake in the Lutour valley. 20 places, open 14
June-11 October.

Bayssellance hut   2651m.
CAF. An old but somewhat improved hut, standing above the foot of the Ossoue glacier on the E side of the Vignemale. 70 places, self-cooking facilities, open 1 July–15 September. Can be reached from Gavarnie or Pont d'Espagne; see under Vignemale.

Brèche de Roland (Sarradets) hut   2587m.
CAF. At the Col des Sarradets and below the Brèche de Roland, the famous gateway in the rock wall above Gavarnie. Base in France for Monte Perdido, Cilindro, Marboré and Ordesa valley. Self-catering facilities, 55 places (nearly always full), open 1 July–15 September. For access, see Monte Perdido.

Espuguettes hut   2027m.

PNP. E of Gavarnie on the Plateau de Pailla, just off the track to the Hourquette d'Alans. Finely situated with a view of the Gavarnie cirque and the more distant Vignemale. 60 places, open 1 July to 15 September.

Gavarnie (Grange de Holle) hut   1480m.
CAF. 50 places, open throughout the year. This valley hut is about 2km. along the road from Gavarnie to the Port de Gavarnie.

Centre d'acceuil des Especières   1850m.
Not a true hut but a pleasant, well appointed building primarily for winter sports visitors. 40 places, full services. Open from end of ski season to end of autumn. About 7km. along road from Gavarnie to Port de Gavarnie.

Spain

The mountain traveller is generally badly served in the matter of huts, though many French huts near the frontier reduce the inconvenience. Dates of opening are subject to alteration if heavy snow persists.

Belagua (Belagoa) hut   1428m.
Local authority. 120 places, full services, open throughout the year. On main Col de la Pierre St. Martin – Isaba road.

Zuriza hut   1227m.
Old frontier guards' quarters converted into a hut; no details.

Atxerito bivouac   1550m.
At head of the Barranco Atxerito, reached by forest road N of Selva de Oza (3km.), and path of 6km. up the valley. SE of the frontier Pic de la Chourique, and 2km. S of the Ansabère needles in France.

Selva de Oza   1140m.
Large organised camping area; covered shelter facilities nearby; open
1 June–15 September.

Piedrafita (Peñalara) hut   2140m.
FEM. A new 'mansion', 200 places, warden and restaurant service.
Situated below the S side of the Balaitous, in the Campo Plano cwm,
and close to the N side of the Respumoso reservoirs. Jeep road access
to below barrage, or on foot from Sallent de Gallego. Old hut on E
side of barrage lake at 2150m.

Delgado Ubedo (Goriz) hut   2250m.
FEM. The old Goriz hut is lower down. About 100 places, warden
and restaurant service, self-catering facilities, open 1 July–30 September. Beneath the S face of Monte Perdido and above the head of
the Ordesa valley. Base for the Perdido massif and the Añisclo canyon. See Monte Perdido.

Old Goriz hut   2160m.
This hut, standing about 500m. distance down the slope from the Delgado hut, is open from June to October. No hut-keeper, no facilities, 15 uncomfortable places.

Ordesa Park bivouacs
Above the N side of the roadhead are two 4-man hovels (marked on RP
mapping) for rock climbers: Tozal del Mallo (1780m.), and Galliñero
(1600m.); both belong to the forestry service, doors unlocked.

In most of the high valleys on the Spanish side of the frontier, usually
close to a road, are several small forestry huts and larger private establishments with cheap facilities ; normally easy access from a village
or hamlet. Several are noted in the guide.

CAMPING

Camping is officially prohibited within the PNP area and there are a
few noticeboards to this effect. Nevertheless there appears to be no
objection to individual tents being pitched, which are seen in all parts
of the park, particularly in the vicinity of huts. Outside the park you
may camp wherever you wish. There are official camping areas in the
lower inhabited valleys. Similar situations obtain in Spain.

FRONTIER CROSSING

If the frontier is crossed by the 5 roads in this area the usual formalities
are observed. Crossing from France into Spain by mountain paths no
longer presents any problem for walkers and climbers. In 1967 agree-

ment was reached between the French and Spanish authorities allowing free passage into Spain by any mountain route to holders of a special card issued by alpine clubs to their members. Parties have crossed the frontier countless times since this date but have never been asked to produce a card; it seems that the Spanish frontier guards, more rarely met now than formerly (except at times in the Basque country) use their common sense in recognizing bona fide mountain travellers. Passage from Spain into France is entirely unrestricted. While there are a number of well spaced frontier stones, there is generally nothing to indicate where the frontier runs. Here and there you may find small notices reading "Reserva Nacional de Caza", ie National Game Reserve, which indicates that you are entering Spain.

LANGUAGES

A working knowledge of French or Spanish is desirable. English may be understood and spoken in the larger hotels and by some people you may meet in the huts but generally it is not understood. French is understood to some extent on the Spanish side of the frontier and vice versa. In France the normal everyday language of the inhabitants is not French. In Haute Soule it is Basque; in the Aspe and Ossau valleys Béarnais is spoken; in the Gave de Pau valley the language is Bigourdan. These tongues are quite unintelligible to a Parisian, but thankfully all also speak French, though not with the accent you may have been taught at school. Similarly, in Spain, the everyday language is Aragonese, not Castillian, though this too is also spoken.

EQUIPMENT

What you should take depends on intentions but it is always better to be over rather than under equipped. The minimum should include good mountain boots, hooded water and windproof anorak, heavy and light sweaters, breeches and heavy woollen stockings and a woollen cap. The growing tendency to wear shorts is fine providing more substantial clothing is carried for a change in conditions. A torch and spare batteries should also be taken; useful in unlit dormitories as well as for signalling in case of serious trouble. A large scale map is essential and a compass useful. In huts blankets are provided but many prefer to take their own lightweight sleeping bag.

More ambitious trips on the higher peaks may call for an ice axe and a rope for rock pitches. Glaciers, with one exception, are of the cirque variety, ie breadth without length. These lie under some of the frontier crests and are snow covered in summer. The exception is the Ossoue glacier on the Vignemale. Its length is modest but it alone falls below the summer snow line. It is also heavily crevassed, but in normal summers all crevasses are well covered and present no problem. While people will be seen to carry crampons there is rarely a need for them.

MOUNTAIN RESCUE

Mountain rescue is well organised on the French side. The service has all the usual equipment for high altitude work, including helicopters, which also carry out routine patrols. The main mountain rescue centre for this area is at Gavarnie, at the S end of the village on the road to the Cirque. Signboarded: Secours en montagne. Flag flying.

Do not call out the Rescue Service unless it is absolutely essential. Apart from involving a lot of people in possibly unnecessary work, it will be extremely expensive for you. When reporting an accident with which the party cannot cope themselves the messenger should mark the exact spot of the injured person on the map and take it with him to the nearest hut or the nearest inhabited valley. The marking of the map can be important. The messenger may have language or other difficulties in giving the exact location of the injured person, and he is likely to be too tired to act as a guide to the rescue team who will wish to set a pace too fast for him.

All huts with keepers hold a certain amount of rescue equipment and are being equipped with radio receiver-transmitters in touch with the Gendarmerie. Search for a telephone in a valley may be a long job but once found the Gendarmerie should be asked for. Unless you are fluent in French, do not try to give details over the phone. Simply say there has been an accident, where you are phoning from and wait for their arrival when you can show the marked map and give details of the injuries. The French service in action impresses with speed and efficiency. The author has no personal knowledge of the service in Spain.

HISTORICAL

Those who have looked at the formidable appearance of the Pic d'Ossau may be surprised to learn that the first known assault on it took place in May, 1552 ; it failed. From the secondhand existing account it is not possible to determine how far from the summit the gentlemen who were bold enough to make the attempt were forced to give up. By 1787 the peak had been climbed by a person or persons unknown, for in that year a cairn was seen on the summit. 10 years later saw the first successful recorded ascent of the peak by Guillaume Delfau and Mathieu, a shepherd. Delfau climbed it for fun - no scientific nonsense about it. He is not known to have made the ascent of any other mountain.

The first great name in the Pyrenees is that of Louis-François Ramond. He came by chance to spend 5 weeks at Barèges in 1787. He had already paid a brief visit to Switzerland and had been fascinated by the mountains and, in particular, glaciers. Ramond did not climb for the sake of climbing but in pursuit of knowledge. He saw himself as something of a philosopher - a fashion of the period. During those 5 weeks he went as far as the Maladeta massif and was the first to reach the summit ridge at over 3000m. He also saw Monte Perdido from a distance but did not then think of climbing it. After writing a book of great interest he returned to the Pyrenees in 1792 for a stay of 8 years. He is popularly remembered as the first man to reach the summit of Monte Perdido during a later visit in 1802, but it was, in fact, climbed a few days before his ascent by the 2 local men he had sent ahead to reconnoitre a route; their names, Laurens and Rondou.

During the first half of the 19th century exploration moved slowly. The Vignemale was climbed in 1835, again by 2 local men, Henri Cazaux and Bernard Guillembet, seeking a route for a client. The latter, having to leave the district, was unable to make the first tourist ascent but the following year Cazaux promised this distinction to the Prince de la Moskowa, the son of Napoleon's Marshal Ney. In the meantime Miss Anne Lister of Shibden Hall, Halifax had arrived at St. Sauveur. This formidable lady, no longer in her youth, was a seasoned traveller. She had 'done' Monte Perdido in 1830 and now learning of the Prince's intention decided to beat him to the summit. With Cazaux as guide, she reached the Pique-Longue, the highest point, on 7 August, 1838.

Cazaux then took the Prince and his brother up by the same route 4 days later, selling them the expedition as a first tourist ascent and telling them - presumably because the tracks of Miss Lister in the snow could not be hid - that she had been taken ill and had not reached the summit. On his return the Prince was quick to publish locally an account of his exploit. Miss Lister, not unreasonably, was vexed and got a lawyer to draw up a document certifying her prior claim, for Cazaux to sign. Threatened with legal action and refusal on Miss Lister's part to pay him, Cazaux signed. This did not prevent the Prince, in the account of his ascent published in 1842, from giving the impression of a 'first' or from making any reference to Miss Lister. By then she could no longer object, having died from the plague in the Caucasus 2 years earlier.

In 1861 Count Henry Russell began a Pyrenean campaign which lasted 43 years. Russell, born in Toulouse, was of Irish descent. His title

24

was a Papal one. He was a romantic and an eccentric and he was in love with the Pyrenees. He explored them from end to end: the number of first ascents which fell to him is astonishing. Never without his sheepskin sleeping bag, he preferred to sleep on the mountainside, and he covered prodigious distances day after day at a time when there were few paths apart from sheep tracks and no maps worthy of the description.

His name is for ever associated with the Vignemale. Becoming tired of the constant trudge to and from Gavarnie, he first had 3 caves hacked out of the rock above the head of the Ossoue glacier at 3200m. Here he spent happy days and nights and received visitors; this was in the 1880s. But by 1887 the snow level of the upper glacier basin had risen and blocked the entrances to his caves. Reluctantly he had 3 more caves excavated near the then foot of the glacier on the track coming up from Gavarnie, but at only 2400m. When he held dinner parties here he always wore full evening dress, so the author was told some time ago by an elderly man who remembered him. In 1889 the local authorities gave him legal title to the whole of the Ossoue glacier and the surrounding peaks of the Vignemale. He was delighted and wrote: It is certainly the highest estate in Europe and, despite its sterility, I would not exchange it for the finest in France.

In 1893 he achieved his final triumph on the Vignemale. He had a cave blasted only 18m. below the highest point, and in 1904, at the age of 70, he spent 17 days on his own mountain and climbed its summit for the last time. His greatest book "Souvenirs d'un Montagnard" describes all his ascents. Written with enthusiasm and not a little exaggeration, it is now very difficult to obtain.

Linked with Russell is the name of Charles Packe, his friend and companion on some of his ascents. Packe was a Leicestershire landowner and a botanist. He did much pioneer work on the Spanish side of the frontier, a region then almost unknown, and in 1862 he published the first "Guide to the Pyrenees" in English, to be followed 4 years later by the first and very accurate map of the Maladeta massif. In 1864 he made what he believed to be the first ascent of the Balaitous, and not by the easiest route, only to find evidence on the summit of an earlier visit. It was later established that this had been made as early as 1825 by an Army Survey team led by 2 young lieutenants, Peytier and Hossard, who, the following year, spent 8 days on the summit in a snowstorm and who got down only with difficulty.

Russell and Packe rarely made true climbs; most were fairly easy scrambles; others began to seek out more interesting routes to the summits. Most notable during the late 19th century was the forcing of the Gaube Couloir on the Vignemale N face, made in 1889 by Brulle, Bazillac, de Monts and the guides Célestin Passet and Salles. This climb, still graded TD, is of 600m., and they found the very narrow upper chimney of the couloir blocked by a large ice-covered boulder. Passet turned it and they completed the climb by a natural staircase of ice. This route was not repeated in its entirety until 1946.

At the turn of the century a new team astonished their contemporaries by the audacity of their exploits – this was the 5 Cadier brothers from the village of Osse in the Aspe valley. A legend in their own life-time, their gaiety shows clearly through their writings. They are associated in particular with the Balaitous where they opened a number of routes of considerable difficulty on the fiercer of the ridges and also a direct route on the W face. An attractive team, admitted by Russell, who abhorred 'acrobatic' mountaineering, as 'model mount-aineers'.

The next great name is that of Dr Jean Arlaud who, in the 1920s and 30s, produced a large number of difficult routes, mainly in the high frontier district to the E of our present area. He was killed on the Gourgs Blancs in 1938. Another great team of the pre-war years was that of Robert Ollivier and Roger Mailly, both still with us. In 1934 they opened their campaign on the unclimbed faces of the Pic d'Ossau. Up to that time all climbing in the Pyrenees had been 'free' climbing; it was this pair who pioneered the use of artificial aids and were thus able to make routes of great difficulty hitherto believed impossible.

Since the war the number of first class climbers has increased rapidly. It would be invidious to mention some names in preference to others. In recent years the more difficult routes have been attempted and ach-ieved in winter, and specialist winter climbing has developed as else-where in mountain regions. For example, in 1971 a party spent 3 days and 2 nights on a winter climb of 600m. upon a face of the Petit Pic d'Ossau.

The reason why no mention has been made of any Spanish climber is simple; Spaniards came relatively late into the field, that is unless we accept the claim of King Pedro III of Aragon to have reached the summit of the Canigou in the Eastern Pyrenees in 1280. His account is rendered dubious by a description of a dragon he found in a tarn on the summit.

FAUNA

Of the more interesting species first place must be given to the Isard, the chamois of the Pyrenees. Slightly smaller than its Alpine cousin, it can be seen at a distance with comparative frequency and just below the snowline in summer. You may expect to see a number of isards any day around the Pic d'Ossau, but they are not easy to pick out as they

26

graze among the rocks. There are herds round the Balaitous and on the high plateau above the Cirque de Gavarnie.

Far more rare is the large European Brown Bear. It has been estimated that about 50 are still to be found in the whole of the Pyrenees; the author has never seen one. Obviously dangerous if attacked or annoyed, it is said that on the first whiff of the approach of man they will make off deeper into the forest, terrified. More jolly little animals are marmots; not native to the Pyrenees, several colonies have been introduced from the Alps during the last 40 years, and they are now well established in several districts; though still fairly rare and not often seen.

The Desman is the rarest of creatures. The size of a large rat with a pointed snout and half-webbed feet, it lives in the banks of streams. It is found only in the Pyrenees and the Caucasus. The Ibex or Bouquetin, once found above the Ordesa valley, has now disappeared, shot out of existence. The Golden Eagle, gone from the Alps, is still to be found, but any large bird seen circling is more likely to be a Griffin Vulture. These are common round the Col du Pourtalet and indeed wherever flocks of sheep are grazing on the high pastures in summer. This great bird with a 2-metre wing span can be seen frequently at close range and is readily identifiable by the white ruff and bare pink neck. The small Egyptian Vulture is a summer visitor. Not as common as the Griffin, it can occasionally be seen, appearing as white from below and with an orange-yellow head. The third and most rare vulture is the Bearded Vulture, or Lammergeyer. About the same size as the Griffin, and distinguishable from it from below by its different silhouette.

FLORA

One need not be a botanist to realise and enjoy the great variety of flowers both in the valleys and on the heights of the Pyrenees. One of the most vivid memories from the author's first visit is of the sea of blue and yellow iris covering the pastures of the upper Gállego valley, S of the Col du Pourtalet. Another is from the pastures at the head of the Ordesa canyon, where, one morning in mid July, the air was thick with the scent of dark rich honey. All who climb to the summits will see the gentians as they pass without, perhaps, distinguishing between the different varieties. The botanist will know that the Pyrenees offer one of the richest fields in Europe for his search for rare specimens, and will make several visits at different times of the year between late April and the end of September.

GRADING OF ASCENTS

These are based on the international system for general mountaineering and rock climbing, as translated from the French. In rising order of seriousness and difficulty the general application is: F, PD, AD, D, TD, ED, etc. The numerical equivalent for strictly rock pitches is: I, II, III, IV, V, VI, etc. Both are qualified for more accuracy by plus (+) or minus (-) signs to indicate high or low in the grade. Many routes in this guide, including most hut walks, etc. are labelled 'ungraded'. Elsewhere in Europe this category is defined as 'elementary' or for 'pedestrians' and is shown by the letters E or P. Traditionally F used to cover this category, but the tendency nowadays is to divorce mountaineering standards from walking and scrambling ones. In general there are no detailed route descriptions above the level of AD+ (III+) in this guide. In British rock climbing parlance this is equivalent to the traditional 'very difficult' grade. F would be equivalent to Bristly Ridge in Snowdonia or Striding Edge on Helvellyn.

TIMES AND DISTANCES

Times are very relative, depending on the age, ability and fitness of the walker. PNP signposts give times to places indicated but tend to be erratic in over and under estimates by a wide margin. Times given will tend to err on the long side; no allowance is made for halts and distances are given in kilometres (km.) only.

LEFT AND RIGHT

(L, R). Unless otherwise indicated, when used with reference to the bank or side of a stream, L and R mean in the direction in which you are moving, up or down, and not as previously stated in relation to the downward flow of the stream. This rule may also apply to other features. Eg. where formerly you went up the L bank of a gully (in reality the R side in ascent), you now go up the R side; and in descent you come down the L side.

NOMENCLATURE

As the frontier runs through many of the summits, these often have both French and Spanish names. Most of these are similar enough to avoid confusion. Because much of the early exploration in Spain was done by Frenchmen, some of the purely Spanish peaks are better known by their French names; eg Monte Perdido is more usually known as Mont Perdu. In such cases both versions are given. Many topographical features have names in the local language. IGN has 'frenchified' them on some maps, giving a standard French rendering which approximates to the local pronunciation. Some recent maps have reverted to local spellings. Similar chopping and changing occurs on the Spanish side of the frontier.

Grand and Petit Pics du Midi d'Ossau from W.

Larrau - Haute Soule

Maps: IGN 50m. n.1447. IGN/RP 50m. n.2. IGN 25m.V n.273. EA 40m. n.201, 227.

Lying in the most eastern part of the French Basque country, this small area differs in character from the rest of the range. It is an area of high wooded hills rather than of mountains proper and is particularly suitable for walkers (Commune de Ste. - Engrâce). The geography of the region is far from simple and a close study of the map is advisable before walks are planned. Rainfall is heavier and more frequent than in other parts of the Pyrenees. After Pierre St. Martin, the only frontier summit to rise above 2000m. is Pic d'Orhy. The old Basque tongue is still widely spoken hereabouts.

There are 2 frontier road crossings in the district: Port de Larrau (1573m.) and Col de la Pierre St. Martin (1760m.). The Spanish map has its own spelling variations of these and other names. The Refugio Belagua is the only large hut in the area, one km. S of the frontier in Spain, on the international road passing over the Pierre St. Martin col. There are several smaller huts, gîtes d'étape, and many shepherds huts.

The region of Pierre St. Martin is world famous for its caves. It is also a winter ski station. For summer visitors there are 4 spectacular gorges running up towards the frontier. These are described from W to E.

Gorges d'Holzarté

From Larrau take a path to the S of the D.26 road and follow it E for about 1.5km., then turn S above the R side of a stream. After about one km. bear up E through woods to pt.766 where, in a clearing, head S for one km; then make a loop, first W then E, before turning S and finally W above the upper end of the gorge. Cross the stream running into the gorge and continue E through woods to contour a spur and so reach the Pont de Pichta. Here the main path turns S towards the frontier above; ignore this. After crossing the bridge, turn L on a path that heads N through woods some distance above the E side of the gorge; join a path leading down to near the junction at the N end of this gorge with that of the Olhadubi. Cross a sensational, aerial foot tread bridge above the latter canyon and follow the path N to the Logibar hut on the D.26 road, 3km. E of Larrau. About $3\frac{1}{2}$ h.

Gorges d'Olhadubi

From the Logibar gîte d'étape, 3km. E of Larrau on the D.26 road.

From the hut follow a path S for 1.5km. on L side of the stream and rising above the ravine walls to where the exposed footbridge is crossed to ascend the Holzarté woods, as taken in descent by the previous walk. Go up a wooded spur to a fork L. This leads SE to the head of the gorge, crossed by a bridge (840m.) beside a shepherds hut (cayolar). Return N above the R side of the gorge, gradually bearing away from the cliffs. The path climbs to near pt.999, then slants NE into woods along a track leading to some cabins. From there a grassy path WNW goes down a spur to the Logibar hut. Round walk, 2½-3h.

Gorges de Kakouéta

From Senta, at the head of a 9km. road (D.113), branching SE from the D.26 about 8km. S of Tardets. At Senta, hut and camping; follow road down the valley for 5.5km. to the Pont d'Enfer. Cross this bridge to a path that winds SSW above the W side of this 4km. long gorge. Continue generally S to cross above its head at pt.952. Over the stream running into the gorge, ascend E for one km. to pt.1227. Now work N along a big path winding through woods above the E side of the gorge for about 2.5km. to where the path runs into a minor road returning E above the valley road to Senta after about 4km. Allow 6h. At the gorge entrance there is a short picnic walk.

Gorges d'Ehujarré

From Senta to the Belagua hut by this gorge. A path runs S through the gorge from Senta. First take a minor road SSW. After 500m. quit it by a path to the R that runs SW then S into the gorge, some 3 km. long. At the upper end follow the path climbing towards the frontier (1.5km.) and rising to Errayzéko Lépoa before it drops to the frontier (1578m.) and down into Spain to meet in a few min. the main Pierre St. Martin road, C.137. Turn R along the road for 2km. to hut (1428m.). About 3h. from Senta.

PIC D'ORHY 2017m.

IGC 2021m. Outstanding viewpoint and the most westerly frontier summit of the Pyrenees rising above 2000m.

From the Port de Larrau. Ungraded. At the frontier road-crossing pt. 1573m. on the D.26, 12km. S of Larrau, follow a path on the Spanish (S) side of the ridge, and climb keeping close to L side of crest for 2 km. to the summit, 1½h. As a return route the D.26 road can be rejoined from the summit by a path along the steep NW ridge, keeping slightly L of the ridge line, down to a narrow, exposed ridge gap. Pass 30m. below this on the French (N) side, ignore the continuation ridge path and descend NE in a small hollow to cross in a few min. a spur on the R. From here descend an improving track soon slanting gently E to join the Larrau road at the Col d'Erroymendi (1362m.). 1¼ h.

OTCHOGORRIGAGNA 1923m.

IGC 1925m. On the frontier 9km. E of Pic d'Orhy. Note, there are communal shelters with no facilities at the Harpia cabin (1250m.), 2.5 km. NNE below summit, and the Ardane cabin (1312m.), 2km. WNW below summit.

From the Logibar hut. Ungraded. A long rural hike over a big vertical interval. Follow path on E side of the Holzarté gorge (see above) as far as the Pont de Pichta. From here climb steeply SSE through the woods then into the open for about 2.5km. to the Pichta Gagnékoa caves. Now bear SE to the frontier at the Uthurourdinétako pass, or Col d'Uthu (1664m.). Do not cross the pass but contour W for almost one km. then turn the foot of a spur and climb S towards the Otchogorri frontier crest for about 500m. Now go SE to the ridge and follow it NE to the summit. About 7 h.

KARST AREA

The area between Pierre St.Martin and the Pic d'Anie (see Lescun Group) is known as a Karst area. The name comes from a place in the Dinaric Alps, Yugoslavia, where this curious limestone formation was first investigated. The surface is bare rock split by deep fissures known as grikes into blocks called clints. Precipitation on the surface drains through the grikes to underground streams and caves. Traversing this area in misty weather can be dangerous, but a waymarked track crosses it. The frontier is ill-defined here and is not shown precisely on maps.

Arette – Pierre St. Martin to Lescun by Col des Anies

Take the access road S through a skitow zone to Pescamou; the frontier ridge of Pic d'Arlas (2044m.) is to the W. Continue briefly to the Pescamou shepherds huts, and here ascend W over grass slopes to the border at the Col de Pescamou (1918m.). Cross into Spain and bear round SW then SE to re-cross the frontier by the Col de Boticotch (1939m.). The waymarked and cairned track continues SE and enters the Karst area. After less than one km. it runs E past cave holes for another km. before bearing SE to attain the Col des Anies (2084m). From this pass proceed eastwards to the end of the Karst area near the very small Lac d'Anie to the R of the track. This pool can easily be missed. Now follow the path NE to the Cap de la Baitch cabin (1689m.) beneath the Pas d'Azuns to the N. After less than 2km., in woods, find a path branching back to the R and follow this, dropping through the woods to the roadhead at

Sanchèse, 4km. from Lescun. Allow 5½h. If this branch path is not taken, the main path through the woods continues for 1.5km. SE to the Refuge de Labérouat and a roadhead, 3.5km. from Lescun.

PIC DU SOUM COUY 2315m.

This limestone summit lies directly N of Col des Anies. It can be tried either from Lescun/Labérouat hut or from Arette–Pierre St. Martin.

From Lescun/Labérouat hut
Normal way, F. Follow Pic d'Anie routes as far as the tiny Lac d' Anie. Branch R on the track to Col des Anies (2084m.), cross it and turn R up a path over scree and boulders to reach any easy chimney. Go up this and on to a second chimney slightly L of the first. Climb it then make for an isolated rock in the scree. Pass beneath it and turn R on to a rising ledge leading to 2 chimneys. Climb the L-hand one on to grass and on up to the summit, about 3-4h. from hut.

From Arette–Pierre St. Martin
Take the route to Lescun by the Col des Anies (above). Just before reaching the col turn L on a path over scree and so join previous way.

East Ridge
AD-. As for the Lescun/Labérouat approaches to the Pic d'Anie normal route, as far as pt. 2015, a little under 2km. beyond the Cap de la Baitch cabin. Leave path and branch W, climbing grass slopes to reach the foot of the E ridge. Begin ascending to R of ridge foot, then turn onto crest itself; it is narrow, none too solid and care must be taken. Go up to 2 rock towers, close together and a little to L of crest. Turn L and climb between the towers to reach a chimney with good holds leading to top of the R-hand tower. From here the ridge widens and rises to the foot of the summit cone. Climb a gully of large boulders leading to the S ridge. At this ridge turn R and go up to top. 3-4h.

Belagua, Ansó and Hecho valleys

Maps: EA 40m. n.201. IGN 50m. n.1447, 1547. IGN 100m.G n.69.

These 3 Spanish valleys run roughly N from the main Jaca–Pamplona road. The Belagua reaches the frontier at the Col de la Pierre St. Martin. Although the roadheads of the Ansó and Hecho are at some distance from the frontier, they give access to some interesting massifs. The upper parts of these 3 valleys are connected by transverse roads.

EZCAURRE   IGC 2049m.

IGN 2047m. A small massif (Peña Ezcaurri) lying between the Belagua valley to the W and the head of the Ansó valley.

From Isaba. Ungraded. A forest road leads E from the village and after 2km. turns SE up the Barroeta valley on the R side of the stream. At the end of this road in 3.5km. climb steeply by a path straightahead to a col (1650m.). Go N up the crest to pt.1703; then bear R and pass to the L of a small tarn – Ibón de Ezcaurre – to continue ascending NE to a saddle between the 2 summits: Ezcaurre W (2002m.) is to the L. Move R along crest to reach the main top. About 4½h. on foot from Isaba. To the SE of the summit is the Aguja de los Pastores (2041m.) – The Shepherds' Needle – with rock climbing routes graded TD.

From Zuriza. Grade, probably PD. Situated at the head of the Ansó valley, Zuriza (1227m., inns and camping) can be reached from Isaba by a road branching E from the main road, 3km. NE of Isaba. In the other direction, follow this road W to a little short of the Collado Arguibiela, one km. Seek out a path on the L, leading up steeply through woods on the NE ridge of Ezcaurre, under Punta Abizondo (1676m.) and a little further SW to the Collado Abizondo (1638m.). From here climb S by one of several steep gullies in order to reach the summit. 2½–3h. from Zuriza.

RALLA DE ALANO   IGC 2167m.

IGN 2159m. The Alano massif lies between the Ansó and Hecho valleys. Fine viewpoint.

From Zuriza. Ungraded. At the head of the Ansó valley, take forest road SE up the Barranco de Petrafixa. A little short of the roadhead, 4km. from Zuriza, at c.1550m., leave the road and follow a marked path on the R, climbing steeply to the Paso de Chandalán (1900m.).

From this gap turn W and contour across the S side of a secondary top (Atxar de Alano, 2099m.), then mount N on grass slopes and rocks to the highest point. 2h. from road. On the N face of this massif there are various rock climbs up to TD- standard.

FORCA   2390m.

There are several summits of almost equal height, the highest being Atxar de Forca. This massif lies SE of the Alano, between the Ansó and Hecho valleys.

From Selva de Oza. Ungraded. This hamlet (1140m.) lies at the head of the Hecho valley road; huge campsite, inn, forest hut, etc. Follow road heading S from hamlet; cross the bridge and 200m. beyond turn R onto a track climbing through woods above the R side of the Estriviella stream. Clamber steeply through a gap and continue E to a shepherd's hut. From here turn SW up a grass slope and ascend to a gap in the summit ridge. Go up the ridge W, over grass and rocks, and cross pt. 2387m. to gain the highest top. 3-4 h. from Selva de Oza.

From Hecho (833m.) by the Hospital valley. Ungraded. Follow road for 2km. up the valley through Siresa (882m.) and for a further 1.5km. Now on the L, a forest road swings back and, passing above Siresa, turns N to enter the wooded Hospital valley. Go up this rough road for about 7km. to its head. From here ascend by a track E, mounting past a hut to the Collado de Lenito de Abajo (1708m.), a saddle in the Forca S ridge. Follow ridge to the Collado de Arriba, a saddle between pt.2105 to the E and the Atxar de Forca to the NW. Ascend latter by passing over pt.2387. 3-4h. from end of forest road.

BISAURIN (VISAURIN)   IGC 2669m.

IGN 2668m. This mountain is close to the Hecho district, but it is elsewhere described in the Aspe group when coming from the French side of the frontier. However, it is a major summit ascended frequently from the Spanish side. Normal route from the Hecho valley, at the Santa Ana bridge, by going E up the R(S) side of the Agüerri valley, forest road then a path, to Dios Te Salve hut (1735m.). Continue to Collado del Foratón (2032m.) at top, then by SW ridge directly to the summit. About $3\frac{1}{2}$ h. from hut.

CASTILLO DE ACHER   IGC 2390m.

Erroneously depicted by IGN as Monte Campanil, 2331m. This bold, monumental limestone peak can be climbed from Selva de Oza at the head of the Hecho valley, by the R(S) side spur of the Espata/Acher valley, crossing over at a forestry hut (rough, 6 places, 1740m.) to S flank of the mountain, and up this to a ridge gap a short distance from the top, 3½-4h. Numerous rock climbs on the N face.

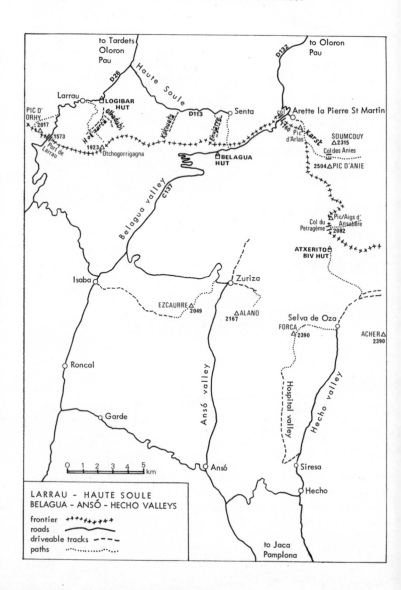

LARRAU – HAUTE SOULE
BELAGUA – ANSÓ – HECHO VALLEYS

frontier   +++++++++++
roads
driveable tracks — — —
paths   ....

Lescun Group

Maps: IGN 50m. n.1447, 1547. IGN/RP 50m. n.3. IGN 25m.V n.273. EA 40m. n.201.

There has been a considerable extension and improvement of roads in the Lescun cirque in recent years. Lescun village (902m.) lies at the end of a short road branching from the N.134, 6km. S of Bedous in the Aspe valley, and on the threshold of a broad and undulating pla-teau ringed on the NW and W by a number of rather distant, strange looking white peaks. This is the Cirque de Lescun. The word 'cirque' is applied in the Pyrenees to a semi-circle of continuous mountain wall at the head of a valley, typified by the famous Cirque de Gavarnie. The Lescun cirque is not strictly in this category.

PIC D'ANIE 2504m.

The most westerly peak to reach 2500m. and the highest of the Lescun group. The easiest approach from Spain, via the Belagua hut, leaves the Pierre St. Martin C.137 road by a marked track E, about 2km. from the pass; this reaches the Col de Pescamou where the Karst area route is joined (see Larrau-Haute Soule). Continue to the Col des Anies, and near here the French route is followed to the summit (3½h. from road). From Arette-Pierre St. Martin by the Karst route, 3h.

Normal French Route
Ungraded, a long mountain walk. A good road leads SW from Lescun for 1.6km., then turns NW to enter the Sanchèse hollow. Just before this, at pt.1110, leave the road and branch R on a path leading up in to woods. A needle-like cliff, the Pic de la Breque, is seen to L across the hollow; in the woods the path is not very distinct in places. Near the top of the wood a path at R-angles is met. Turn L along it and rise through pasture up a broad valley to reach the Cabane de la Baitch (1689m.). Here the Pic de Contende rises to the L(S). The path now ascends on the R side of the stream, then crosses to the L side and mounts more steeply through a gap to the miniscule Anie tarn, when the Pic d'Anie is seen ahead and L. The path winds up SW, away from the Col des Anies, through a curious field of chaotic limestone pits and cracks, then begins a gentle slant across the N face - now seen to be composed of great slopes of scree; a gigantic slag heap. A monolith stands on the slope above the path, which winds round to the W face and, a little more steeply, over broken rock to attain the top

Aiguilles d'Ansabère from the SE. S peak (L) and N peak (R).

from the SW (about 5h.). Pau is visible in clear weather. All the more important peaks to the E are too far away to make the view particularly interesting.

Descent by Vallon d'Anaye   Grade, F
This includes a great deal of scree-glissading - very bad for the boots. From the summit go down the easy E ridge and move on to its N flank at c.2300m. Proceed in same direction until a gully of loose boulders is reached to the R. Go down it, on to the Col de Contende, a depression between the latter and Anie. From here descend into the Anaye valley over loose boulders and scree, then grass slopes taken obliquely towards the SE and so to an obvious path coming up the valley. Go down the valley path E, on the L side, until it passes below the needle cliff and round the N edge of the Sanchèse hollow to rejoin the outward route at pt. 1110. About $3\frac{1}{2}$-4h. in descent to Lescun.

Note: car drivers can go up the little service road from Lescun to the Labérouat hut (1442m.); from there by the GR10 path through the Azuns wood to join the normal route; saves $1\frac{1}{4}$h.

LE BILLARE 2309m.

The Billare with the Petit Billare appear as one when seen from Lescun, to which it is the nearest peak.

Normal Route. Ungraded. From Lescun follow the Anaye valley descent (above) in reverse, and cross the stream to the L side to reach the Anaye huts (1513m.). From here strike up the hillside obliquely SW over tiring grass slopes towards a depression in the crest of the long W ridge. Loose boulders and scree are encountered below the crest. At c.2080m. on the ridge follow the crest line over broken ground to the summit. The true summit is far from clear, being large and with a curious depression in the centre of it suggesting the bed of a tarn or perhaps a shallow crater. 4h. from Lescun. Across the Anaye valley, Pic d' Anie appears as a shapely cone, mildly impressive above its great slopes of scree. The view E is similar to that from the Anie.

PIC D'ANSABÈRE 2360m.

Sp. Petretxema. Not to be confused with the spectacular adjoining rock Aigs. d'Ansabère (N pt.2377m., S pt.2271m.). The last part of the Lescun approach above the Col de Petragème (Port d'Ansó) is easily reached from the Spanish side; Zuriza to Linza biv.hut (1720m.), then by waymarked path E ($2\frac{3}{4}$h. from hut).

Normal route. Ungraded. From Lescun take the road SW which is part of the HRP. It zigzags across the entrance to the Sanchèse hollow and

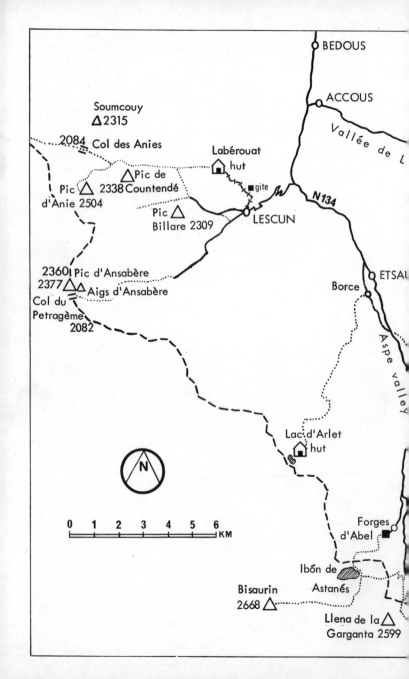

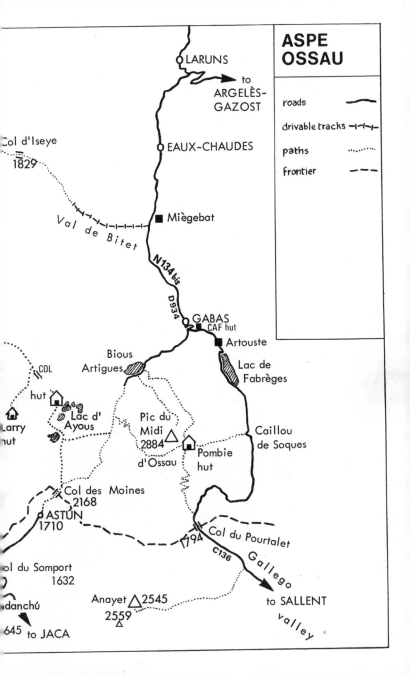

reaches the Gave (stream) at the Pont Lamareich (960m.). The bed is followed in woods to where the road ends just short of the Pont Lamary clearing (1171m.), 7 km. from Lescun. Beyond the bridge rise gently over pasture with the unmistakable Aigs. d'Ansabère, magnificent rock needles, seen ahead in the distance. After passing a shepherd's hut, the path bears L to cross the stream and ascends through woods into the Val d'Ansabe. On reaching the Cabanes d'Ansabe, bear R (L for HRP) and climb under the S face of the Petite, or Aig. S d'Ansabère, to the Col de Petregème (2082m.) at the frontier. The final slope to the pass is bouldery. Cross into Spain and turn R (N) to ascend the last 300m. of fairly steep scree and boulders to the summit of the Pic. 4-5h. from the Pont de Lamareich.

This longish walk with its mixture of woods and pasture is more than rewarded by the spectacle of the Ansabère needles. At the summit, parties on the Aig.N can be seen to advantage. As mentioned in the introductory notes to the guide these needles have a tragic history. The first attempt on the Aig.N was made in 1923 by Armand Calame and Lucien Carrive. On the ascent the rope broke and Carrive fell to his death. In spite of this Calame continued alone and reached the top. On the descent he too fell and was killed. A friend of the author was also killed on this needle in 1967 when attempting a solo ascent. In March 1970 tragedy struck again. Baudéan and Garrotté completed their ascent of the Aig.S but were overtaken by a storm on the descent. Garotté fell and was killed. His companion was left hanging from their rope for nearly 3 days before he was rescued; this was in winter. There have been subsequent dramatic accidents.

The original ascent of 1923 was made on the short W face of the N needle, facing the Pic; it is graded VI-. Longer routes are on the NE and E faces; one of sustained difficulty and 200m. is graded ED- with an A3 artificial pitch. Others on the E face have the same grading. While there is one route on the Aig.S graded only AD, it is subject to rock falls and has pitches of bad rock and cannot be recommended. On the S needle other routes , up to 350m., are graded TD or harder; the S pillar is bolted for over 200m.

Aspe Group

Maps: IGN 50m. n.1547. IGN/RP 50m. n.3. IGN 25m. V n.273. EA 40m. n.201, 25m. n.202.

The main group forms a semi-circle, the limestone Cirque d'Aspe, round the head of the Aspe valley, 5-6 km. SW of the Col du Somport, so that it is really in Spain and the true name of the group is Sierra de Aisa. Here the frontier lies N of the watershed. There are notable outliers, the most prominent being Bisaurin about 6km. NW.

PIC D'ASPE 2645m.

Sp. Pico de la Garganta. IGC 2646m. Motoring climbers can now get up this mountain in 2½h. from the Tobazo roadhead (skiing development, 1900m.) above Candanchú on the Spanish side of the Somport pass. Snow lies until mid summer and some of the slopes are steep. To a col in NE ridge near the Tuca Blanca (2323m.), then by L side of ridge with turning movement R at the top.

Normal Route

Ungraded. 8km. S of Urdos on the N.134, start from a bridge at pt. 1405 on a switchback section; holiday centres above and below road here. Cars may be parked to R of road about 200m. distance beyond the bridge. From here the Aspe group is clearly seen to the S. Much of the route is not covered by IGN mapping.

The path, rather vague but marked by small cairns, leaves the road just below the bridge and goes S along a grassy crest towards a wood. On entering the wood, the path is broad and clear. At the end of the wood it rises gently over swelling pasture and reaches a kind of small untidy cirque with a cliff rising steeply to the R. The track, not very evident, bears to the L (ignore another going R) in the cirque and mounts SE over loose boulders and scree to a point just below the crest, which is the frontier. The path does not cross it, but curves R on a broad shelf round the inside of the cirque. After passing a large overhang it doubles back to the S and rises over the frontier crest through a small gap in the rock. This leads to a large open flattish area sloping eastwards from a skyline, an area called Causiat. Turn half R towards the skyline following line of small cairns. All this ground is full of pits (caving) and is dangerous in mist. A straight line between some cairns will lead you into more than one of them.

When the skyline is reached it is found to be the eastern crest of the Cirque d'Aspe. Follow the crest S for about one km., then cross it and go down towards the head of the cirque obliquely so as to lose as little height as possible over boulders and snow patches. The peak with 2 summits is seen above the SE arc of the cirque. Due S is a domed top, Llena de la Garganta (2599m.), and between it and our peak is the Brèche d'Aspe (2425m.). Make for this col, below which there are usually steep snow slopes. On reaching it, turn L and, keeping on the R (S) side of the crest, go up to the first summit. The second and the highest point is gained in a few min. by crossing a gap. 4-5h. from main road.

Return by the Pas d'Aspe
Grade, PD-. Reverse the outward route to the floor of the cirque. Drop down the floor northwards by rocky terraces and head for the R bank of the stream when it appears. Still in the cirque, cross to the L bank and, on approaching the low northern wall of the cirque, the frontier, in which there is an obvious central gap, re-cross to R side. Passing through the gap the path drops steeply in a long narrow gully of large boulders. This is the Pas d'Aspe (1675m.), graded II+, but not presenting any difficulty to the experienced mountain walker. At the foot of the gully a clear path leads across the R-hand slope of the valley. It enters a wood, bears round to the R and emerges on the pasture slopes where the lower part of the outward route is joined. $3\frac{1}{2}$h. from summit to main road.

BISAURIN 2669m.

Fr. Visaurin. IGN 2668m. See also entry in Belagua, Ansó and Hecho valleys section. The highest top of the Aspe group.

Normal Route. Ungraded. On the N.134 road, about 8km. S of Urdos, at pt.1327, a short lane on R branches down to a parking area above the stream. PNP map displayed on board. From this spot, known as Sansanet, take the path marked by red and white horizontal bars that drops to the stream and crosses by a footbridge. On the other side bear R and follow the path N up through woods. Soon join the HRP trail mounting W over grass slopes to the frontier (marked) and carry on westwards to a grassy saddle from which the Ibón de Astanès is seen below, straightahead. Follow the path down towards the lake; about 250m. from it look for the beginnings of a path to the L(S) marked by small cairns which starts near the meagre ruins of a small hut. Take this path up and over a rocky limestone crest. It leads down to a grassy valley running E-W. The path and cairns disappear. Note carefully where this path ends for it is not easy to find in the reverse direction. Turn W along the valley for about 300m. and look for a path rising over the southern slopes. This ascends to a second and higher rocky crest and through a gap in it to a very beautiful cirque, Valle de los Sarrios, a level lawn-like expanse with 2 or 3 rock monoliths in its centre. Pass these and follow a path leading up the W side of the cirque. This swings R to a low saddle, from which the Bisaurin is seen straightahead at the end of a valley. The path drops slightly down the valley, leaves a gap (Puerto de Aragues) on the L then starts to rise towards a broad gully falling from the Bisaurin. The path keeps on the R side of stream coming down the gully until it reaches its head. Here it turns L and starts to ascend obliquely across the scree slopes of the mountain. On nearing the first summit (2654m.) the path reaches boulders. The second and higher summit is only a few m. from the first. About $5\frac{1}{2}$ h. from carpark. The view E in clear weather includes Monte Perdido. To the S the distant Sierra Moncayo, S of the Ebro valley, can sometimes be seen.

ROUTES BETWEEN THE ASPE AND OSSAU VALLEYS

By the Col d'Iseye   1829m.

About 2 km. S of Bedous village in the Aspe valley a side road to the E leaves the main road for Accous (480m., one km.), an ancient village which was once the "capital" of the semi-autonomous Aspe valley. It lies at the entrance to the Berthe valley, penetrating ESE. The old cart track up this valley is now a good road for about 4.5km. to a pt. a little short of the first climb in zigzags through a wood. Blue paint splashes on rocks, etc. mark the way to the col.

Leave the village by the small road E and after one km. cross the Cha-guye bridge (562m.) to the R side of the valley. Continue at length between stone walls and hedges with patches of woodland to a sharp bend R (c.860m.). Round this bend, on R side of streambed, go off L (E) up a narrow track to climb by zigzags through a wood and crossing the base of a ridge SE. The path then rises over pasture (shepherd's hut to R); it disappears but paint splashes mark the way. Ascend more steeply to find the path at R-angles running across a low rock ridge. Turn L(N) along it and when a second hut (Escurets) is approached, turn R and rise over grass to the col.

On the other (E) side the path drops and passes to the R of the Cabane Laiterine, then goes SE down the R bank of a stream. It descends through a wood, crosses the stream and passes another hut; more zigzags then woods to reach a bridge. Cross this to a rough road going down the R bank of the Bitet stream, through woods to reach the road in the Ossau valley just above a power station at Miégebat, 5km. N of Gabas. About, 6–7 h.

By the Col d'Ayous   2185m.

In the Aspe valley leave the N.134 road at Pont de Cebers (637m.), 1.5km. S of Etsaut, and follow the track (GR10 waymarks throughout) rising on the E side of the valley to pt.788, where it turns sharp E on a remarkable path hewn out of an almost vertical rockface. This is the Chemin de la Mâture, made in the 1670s for bringing logs for ships' masts down from the forests above. At that time Louis XIV and his minister Colbert were carrying out a programme of expansion of the French navy. This path climbs above a gorge, on whose opposite side stands the now abandoned Fort d'Urdos. The track reaches a farm building in a small clearing (Perry) where spring water can be obtained from a pipe in an adjacent field. A level stretch of over one km. ends in a sharp rise where the path is joined by a secondary path from Etsaut. Follow the path E and after 2 bridges wade a stream. The path turns SE and, leaving the woods, reaches the Cabane de la Baight de St. Cours (1560m.). From here the track turns S and mounts gently through open pasture to pt.1888, where it zigzags SW to join a path coming from the Refuge de Larry. Turn SE to the Col d'Ayous; magnificent view of the Pic du Midi d'Ossau. Follow the track down to the first of the Ayous lakes and the Refuge d'Ayous (1982m.). About 7h. from Pont de Cebers.

Two tracks lead from the hut to the valley of the Gave de Bious. One runs S, first climbing a little, then skirting Lac Bersau to join the path coming up the Bious valley towards the Col des Moines. Follow the path down this valley, NE to the Lac de Bious-Artigues, and the road down to Gabas in the Ossau valley.

The other, shorter, path from the hut passes N of Lac Gentau and Lac Roumassot. It drops easily down and passes through woods to the Bious valley near Pont de Bious, a little over one km. from the Lac de Bious-Artigues.

By the Col des Moines   2168m.

At the Col du Somport the new road in Spain to the developing skiers' resort of Astún considerably alters and shortens the old track to the Col des Moines. The 2.5km. road ends in a carpark at the Casa de Astún, 1710m. (bus service). From here follow a path N to the Ibón de Escalar (2078m.), pass round its NW end and bear due E to climb to the Col des Moines, less than 2km. from the carpark.

Cross the saddle into France, descend NE and bear R to reach the Lac Casterau, which is passed on its S side. Continue on the well-worn path, leaving 2 shepherds huts to your R, and reach a footbridge over the Bious stream. Cross to the R side and follow the track over flat pastures to the Pont de Bious. Cross to the L side of the stream and follow the road to the Bious-Artigues reservoir and the roadhead above the dam. Café and carpark. A road runs down from the dam to Gabas and the main road in the Ossau valley, a further good hour's walk. About $4\frac{1}{2}$ h. from Astún to the Bious-Artigues reservoir.

Bisaurin from the NW.

Ossau

Maps : IGN 50m. n.1547. IGN/RP 50m. n.3. IGN 25m.V n.273.
EA 25m. n.202. The Ossau valley is dominated by the Pic du Midi
d'Ossau, rising W of the road between Gabas and the frontier in the
upper valley. So important and interesting is this peak that lesser summits in the immediate vicinity are generally ignored except for one
impressive mountain across the frontier in Spain.

PIC DU MIDI D'OSSAU 2884m.

Many find this the most satisfying peak in the whole of the Pyrenees,
both from its unique appearance and by reason of the magnificent scrambles and rock climbs it offers on granite. Like the Matterhorn, it
stands alone, a rock peak rising from pastures and with no satellites of
any consequence crowding it or spoiling its silhouette. It has 2 obvious
summits, the Grand Pic and, to the W, the Petit Pic, separated by a
deep cleft known as the Fourche (2705m.). There are 2 other summits,
not immediately apparent, on its SE side; Pointe d'Aragon and Pointe
Jean Santé. Altogether there are over 80 routes and numerous variations. The Pombie hut stands beneath the SE (Pombie) wall. This hut
is the starting point for a large number of climbs and scrambles, including the easiest route of ascent on the E face.

APPROACHES TO THE REFUGE DE POMBIE 2031m.

All 3 paths below have been improved and widened by the PNP.

From Bious-Artigues - reached by a side road SW from Gabas;
carpark just above the dam, café. A PNP signpost in the carpark indicates the start of the path to the Col de Suzon and the hut. This wide
path does not need detailed description. Starting in woods, it soon
ascends to the down-like Col Long de Magnabaight, then turns S up
the long Magnabaight valley, first on the R side then on the L of the
stream. It attains the Col de Suzon (2127m.), a pass on the spur falling from the E face of the Pic d'Ossau. S of the col the path drops,
passes below the towering Pombie wall, and winds through a sea of
gigantic boulders, the Grande Raillère. It finally emerges a few m.
from the little Lac de Pombie; the hut stands above the E end of this
tarn. 3h.

From Caillou de Soques. At a point 9 km. S of Gabas in the
Ossau valley on the N.134 bis road (D.934), the road (otherwise fairly

straight) makes a sharp V-turn. This is at a point level with an entrance W to the Val de Pombie, a spot known as the Caillou de Soques (1392m.). Cars can be parked to the L of the road. The E face of the Pic d'Ossau is seen in the gap of the Val de Pombie. Drop into the main valley and cross the stream by a footbridge. The path W up the Pombie side valley is so broad and obvious that no description is needed. It leads directly to the hut in about 2 h.

From the Anéou pastures - open pasture W of the N.134 bis road (D.934) just N of the frontier. About 1.3 km. short of the Col du Pourtalet, a short track leaves the road opposite a small concrete hut and drops to a carpark W of the road. The path leaves the carpark, crosses a stream (bridge) and climbs towards the Pic d'Ossau, whose summits can be seen to the NW above a screening grass ridge. The obvious path goes up to this ridge in long zigzags; Col du Soum. On the other side it runs N, almost level to the hut. $1\frac{1}{2}$ h.

GRAND PIC 2884m.

East Face Normal Route.
Grade, F+. From the Pombie hut go back along the path to the Col de Suzon, then follow a track on the spine of the grass ridge rising to the E face (2345m.). Climb the first chimney in the face; all iron stanchions have been removed but there are good holds. At the top move out L up a short sloping slab with a moveable wooden peg which can be placed, if desired, in any of several holes. A well-worn path then turns R, rising across the face to the foot of a second chimney, rather longer than the first and with good holds; one iron peg remains near the top on the R. At the top of this chimney the path continues to rise across the face and almost reaches the N face. A cairn some 30-40m. from it indicates the entrance to the L of a gully of easy rock which leads to the third, so-called, chimney; more of a long sloping groove. A few pegs remain here but the ascent is quite easy without them. At the top note an iron post with a pointed indicator (2657m.). This is to mark the start of the route for the descent which, in mist, is not too easy to find.

The ascent now eases to a gentle slope over the wide "roof" of the peak, known as the Rein de Pombie, littered with broken rocks and crossed by a large number of tracks, all of which converge on the first summit. But, from the head of the groove, bear half L until the edge of the S cirque is reached. From here a narrow shattered ridge leads down to the tower of Pointe d'Aragon. Across the cirque the long fierce-looking Peyreget ridge falls from the Petit Pic, unseen from here. Follow the edge of the S cirque to the first summit, Pointe de France (2878m.). This point is the apparent summit of the peak when seen from Bious-Artigues. The true top, Pointe d'Espagne (2884m.) is seen about 100m. away. Reach it by

Pic du Midi d'Ossau from the W; at Lacs d'Ayous on GR 10.

a very narrow ridge, cut on both sides by 2 steep gullies. Care should be taken here, but a rope is not needed in summer. 3-3$\frac{1}{2}$h. from hut. Starting from Bious-Artigues to reach the Col de Suzon, about 5$\frac{1}{2}$h. to summit.

The view to the E is very fine. Across the Ossau valley the Val d'Arrious opens with the graceful pyramid of Pic Palas at its head and, to its R, the more massive Balaitous; further R the distant Vignemale.

For the descent only those familiar with the mountain should attempt one of the gullies on the E face, all of which require rope work and some knowledge of route finding.

North Face.

Grade AD-. The easiest climb on this face; rope needed. Two starts are possible. (1) From Pombie hut take path to the Suzon col, as for the normal route. On N side of col, quit the main path and trend L along an indistinct path traversing grass slopes at the head of the Magnabaight valley, beneath the crest rising to the E face. Make for a point below a gap in the Moundelhs ridge running down the W side of the Magnabaight valley. Climb steeply to this gap, the Br. de Moundelhs (2122m.). From this point a massive buttress is seen to the L, thrusting out from the N face of the mountain. Descend steeply from the gap, turn sharp L and climb to the Br. des Autrichiens, which lies behind the buttress and from which the N face route starts. 1$\frac{3}{4}$h. Or (2) From the Bious-Artigues carpark above the dam follow the path on S side of the lake until a broad track branches L through a wide clearing. The track enters woods and climbs steadily through them for 1$\frac{3}{4}$h. and finally emerges into the open but deep valley above the R side of a stream. The western slopes of the Moundelhs ridge rise above it to the E. The path bears round R, when the N face is seen. Ahead is the large buttress separated from the face by the Br. des Autrichiens. To reach this gap, the buttress can be turned either to the R or L, the path forking below it. About 3h.

From the Br. des Autrichiens the line starts a little below and to L of gap when looking upwards. Climb a slab. Above, move R and, after climbing a short easy gully, make a rising traverse across the face from E to W. A short easy chimney is reached and, above it, a path continues in the same direction but rather more steeply. So reach a gap between a wall L and a gendarme R of the path. Beyond this gap turn L and climb the flank of a buttress. Turn R and cross a gully (stonefall possible). The path then climbs a slope of boulders and reaches a point where one track continues across the face to the Fourche and the other, which is taken, turns L up over terraces of boulders. Turn L and cross beneath a chimney, then cross a minor ridge and reach the foot of a gully. Climb this and gain the northern side of the Rein de Pombie (see normal route). Cross it and reach the Pointe de France and Pointe d' Espagne. About 4 h. from Br. des Autrichiens.

PETIT PIC 2807m.

Peyreget (South) Ridge.
Normal route, grade AD-. Although the grading is the same as for the N face above, it is somewhat easier. From the Pombie hut follow path along S side of lake and continue W to the Col de Peyreget (2300m.), passing the little upper Pombie tarns. This col is at the foot of the ridge. In the other direction it rises slightly S to the Pic de Peyreget (2478m.) in about 20 min. This minor top gives a very fine view of the SE face of the mountain. Isards are often seen here.

At the col cross to W side and turn R under the crest (grass). A path rises by terraces to a ridge gap; there are 2 gaps a few m. apart. Take the second one, go through it and descend about 25m. in the upper part of a long steep gully falling to the Grande Raillère. On the L will be found a cairn-marked track coming down beneath the ridge. The track winds up this flank, finally attains the ridge crest and crosses it by a cairned-marked gap. On the other side take a short ledge ending near the Western couloir - a broad gully of rocks. Climb to the gully head and reach the crest again. Follow it for a few m. then move L onto the R flank of a wide gully of boulders, narrowing towards its head. Cross the gully and climb it, keeping to the L side, and at the head cross R to a small notch in the main ridge. Pass through it and drop to a small platform at the foot of a steep chimney. Climb the chimney (30m., III-). After 20m. a slight overhang is turned on the L, and the chimney above is resumed. At the top a few m. of broken rock slopes lead to summit. From hut, 3-4 h. The view is rather restricted to the NE by the wall of the Grand Pic.

POINTE D'ARAGON 2715m.

Normal Route.
Grade, PD. From the Pombie hut follow the path round N side of lake and at a point near the end of it turn R on to the Grande Raillère. Go up laboriously in the centre of this steep boulder river with unstable blocks of all sizes; good prospects for ankle-twisting. The upper part of this zone is divided by a massive buttress. L of the buttress it narrows to form a steep gully rising to the Fourche, the deep gap between the Petit and Grand Pics. R of the buttress it rises to the South Cirque. At the buttress foot move R and cross the R-hand branch; beware of falling stones. Go up the far edge under sloping rock ledges. Bear L towards

the Aragon tower. Leave the terraces and turn L. Traverse a short, easy slab and reach the foot of a short chimney. Climb it for about 10m. then exit R by climbing a slab. So reach a small rock balcony at the base of the final tower, pierced by a hole. Enter the hole and climb a totally enclosed vertical chimney. There are good holds and enough light from the opening at the top. The exit is at the summit of the tower and is very narrow. Sacks have to be left below or hauled up inside the chimney. 3-4h. from hut.

From the summit the view of the imposing S wall of the Grand Pic is very fine. A traverse of the narrow ridge running to the Grand Pic, although only graded locally PD-, is a little complicated and should not be tried without prior study of the route details (information in hut); rope essential. The Pointe Jean Santé (2506m.) is seen below the Aragon tower to the SE. First climbed by J. Santé solo in 1927, it may be ascended by a variety of routes, none easy, and all but 2 are either graded TD or ED.

Note on Rock Climbs

The classic routes opened by Robert Ollivier and Roger Mailly in the 1930s include, on the Petit Pic, the NW Face (TD), NE Face (TD) and W Face (D). On the Grand Pic the NW Spur (TD+). In 1955 the Ravier brothers made a route on the SW Face (TD). In 1959, Patrice de Bellefon, Jean Ravier and others opened up a route on the S Pillar (ED-). There is a large number of routes of varying difficulty on the great Pombie wall that looms up menacingly above the hut.

Walk round the mountain

A classic walk, easy, varied and interesting, revealing the very differing aspects of the Pic d'Ossau. Conveniently started from either the Pombie hut or Bious-Artigues.

From the hut take the path to the Col de Peyreget (Petit Pic normal route, above). Cross the col and follow the path descending W. This reaches a fairly large area of big boulders through which a way is picked gingerly, guided by rather faint and scarce paint markings. At the foot of the boulders take a faint path bearing L, which drops down to skirt the Lac de Peyreget on its S side. Continue NW along a well marked path. This soon zigzags down to the broad valley of the Bious stream, and on reaching the valley is joined by the path coming from the Col des Moines and the Lacs d'Ayous; signpost. Turn R through flat pastures on the R bank of the stream and cross it by a footbridge. Continue through woods on L bank, re-cross stream and continue on a broad track to the Bious-Artigues lake. Skirt its S side to reach the dam and carpark. From here take the path to the Pombie hut by the

Magnabaight valley and the Col de Suzon, described above. About 7h.

Variation, more circuitous but less rough. From the Pombie hut follow the main path S (route from the Anéou pastures in reverse) over the Col du Soum de Pombie (2129m.) and turn R on a good, almost level path running across the S face of the Pic Peyreget to the low Col de l'Iou (2194m.); here the path turns N and drops to the Lac de Peyreget. This is an easy stroll and avoids the field of large boulders on the W side of the Col de Peyreget.

ANAYET 2559m.

This graceful pointed peak is in Spain, roughly halfway between the Somport and Pourtalet roads and about 4km. S of the frontier. There are 2 distinct tops, one km. apart: Pico de Anayet (NE, 2545m.) and Vertice de Anayet (SW, 2559m.). The Pico is the chief attraction.

Normal Route, grade PD-. From France, cross the Col du Pourtalet and continue down the newly aligned road for nearly 2km. to the now invisible former site of an old inn (Casilla P.C. on maps) on R. Further down on R are 2 isolated trees a short distance from the road.

From this site cross the stream and rise over grass slopes towards the SW. This line brings you to the entrance of the broad Culivillas valley with a stream coming down from the W. Bear R up the valley, keeping high above the stream and roughly parallel to a ridge along N side of the valley. The path is frequently vague in long dry slippery grass; gradually it approaches the ridge to the N and finally reaches it at a buttress. At the buttress foot turn R on to a level plateau containing the 2 Anayet tarns. The Pico rises on the far side and to the N is a striking view of the Pic d'Ossau.

Cross the plateau S of the tarns to the foot of a gap in the SW ridge of the Pico. Climb over red rocks to the low col (2404m.) and cross to its W side. Turn sharp R and climb rocks to the foot of a short easy chimney. Climb it, at the top move R, cross a slab and reach a ledge. From here an easy gully leads to the summit. $3\frac{1}{2}$-4h. from Col du Pourtalet. The view S is dominated by the massive Collarada (2886m.) in an area seldom visited and noted for its wilderness quality. The higher top of Anayet is easily gained along the main ridge in 30 min.

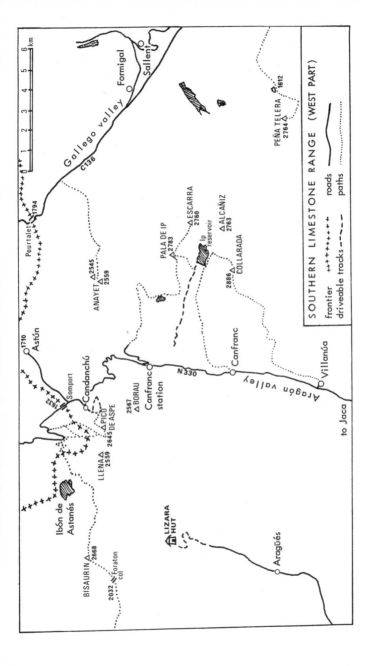

SOUTHERN LIMESTONE RANGE (WEST PART)

frontier ++++++++
driveable tracks -----
roads
paths ·········

Southern Limestone Range

Maps: IGN 50m. n.1648. IGN 100m.G n.70. EA 25m. n.202.
Characteristic and arid barrier sub-range in Spain, extending W-E for
over 30km. It is cut into 2 sections by the Gallego (Tena) valley;
only the Tendeñera ridge lies E of this division. The main summits are
fairly remote and constitute adventurous expeditions.

PEÑA COLLARADA 2886m.

At the W end of the range, between the Aragón and Gallego valleys,
5 km. E of Canfranc. No huts in the vicinity. Though it can be reached from Canfranc, the easier but longer route is from Villanúa, 4
km. S of Canfranc on the Col du Somport - Jaca road. Henry Russell
observed that from Villanúa one could ride on horseback to a point
only 30 min. walk from the summit. He took a more arduous route on
his claimed first ascent in 1876.

From Villanúa, turn SE from the main road on to a road that crosses the river, then take a L fork due E along a service road to a big
bend at the entrance to a side valley. At this point a track goes off
making a higher loop, then climbs N above the road to enter woods
about 2km. from the village. Continue at a moderate angle, gradually to a heading E, and enter the valley of the Barranco de la Trapa.
After some 700m. distance a track forks L and climbs steeply out of the
valley. It bears L and passes a shepherd's hut, heading E again before
turning N to reach higher up the Fuente de los Campanales (c.2460m.)
spring. This point is about one km. W of the summit. Fork R and go
up steeply over boulders to the top. Below, to the NE, lies the great
Circo de Ip, holding the Ip reservoir. About 8h.

From Canfranc Village. Ungraded. Do not confuse Canfranc
village with Canfranc station (Los Arañones), 3.5km. N of the village.
At N end of the village a track leads E, over the river, by the Puente
de los Peregrinos (Pilgrims' Bridge). After the bridge turn L and continue N above the river for 750m. distance, then take a side track R
(ENE), passing under the railway and climbing high above the L side of
the Barranco de Ip. Continue and go through woods for about 2 km.
The track emerges on pastures, high above the cliffs bordering the stream, and progresses into the great Circo de Ip. Pass buildings connected with the dam at the NW end of the reservoir, ascend to the S end
of the dam and follow a track along the SW edge of the reservoir as far
as a hollow opening S. From here climb by a steep path SW to Collado

de Ip (2590m.). Cross this saddle, turn R and go up to the summit. Allow 7-8h.

PALA DE IP 2783m.

Crowning point of the massive wall on the N side of the Circo de Ip.

From Canfranc Station. Ungraded. Follow the main road N, cross the railway where it emerges from the Somport tunnel and take the first side road R; this crosses the river then turns S for a short distance before looping back on itself. Follow this road N, climbing for 1.5km. Turn R and enter the Izas valley at a place called Fuente de Coll Ladrones. The track fades into a path; go along this for a little over 3km. near the R side of the stream. Pass a cabin seen to the L; soon afterwards, leave the path going up the valley and turn sharp R on to a lesser path that climbs SW to a small cirque and leads to a shepherd's hut (Vuelta de Iserias). From here ascend with increasing steepness to a headland (2293m.) lying NE of the Ibón de Iserias, seen in a hollow below. Continue the ascent S along a crest to pt. 2622. Now go E along the undulating summit ridge for about 1.5km. to attain the top. About 6h.

PICO ESCARRA 2760m.

This summit stands 2km. NE of the reservoir in the Circo de Ip, and ESE of the Pala de Ip. It can be reached by following the crest of the ridge from the Pala de Ip, vague track in parts, for a distance of 2km. The big top at the back of the cirque, SE of the reservoir, is the Pala de Alcañiz (2763m.).

SIERRA TELERA

A section of the southern limestone ridge, lying roughly E-W between the Aragón and Gallego valleys. It is about 4km. in length, with summits of over 2700m. It has a N face riven by a series of gullies and ridges. The highest point is the Peña Telera.

PEÑA TELERA 2764m.

The most easterly summit on the Telera ridge. There is an open forestry hut with summary equipment at 1600m. on the jeep road beyond the turning to the tarn (see below). The long N face offers a selection of rock climbs, all but 2 graded D or above. The latter are the Corredor del Collado, AD+, a relatively short gully rising E of the Peña summit and to the W of the Brecha de Telera (normal route); the other is the Gran

Diagonal, AD+, a longer climb, starting to the W of the Corredor de Collado and reaching the E shoulder of the Peña. The big central groove in the N face just R of the summit line (650m., ED-) is long and with much bad rock.

From Piedrafita. Grade, PD. Piedrafita-de-Jaca village is reached from the Col du Pourtalet – Biescas road (C.136) by a short side road brenching W, 1.5km. S of Saqués above the long Bubal reservoir. At the entrance to the village (1242m.) follow an unmade road leading L. It forks: R to Tramcastilla village, L (WNW) for the Ibón de Piedrafita. Go L and follow the jeep track for 2km. to the forest exit and outfall stream (c.1500m.). A piste track goes up this SW, passing a fine man-made shelter bivouac, to the tarn (1612m.) which is contoured on the SE side. Continue SW up the cwm ahead and near the top climb steeply to a scree/rubble gully, possibly snow-filled, which leads to the Brecha de Telera (2450m.). Cross this gap and bear R (W), keeping under a wall until a gap is reached on R. Continue up this on the W flank of the Peña Parda (2657m.) and turn L (N) to follow a broad ridge to the summit. About 4h. from Piedrafita.

TENDEÑERA 2853m.

The Sierra de Tendeñera lies S of the Vignemale massif, between the Gallego (Tena) (W) and Ara (E) valleys, opposite the W entrance to the Ordesa park. It is a fairly level ridge, 10km. in length W-E. At the W end is the Peña Blanca (2558m.) and Peña Sabocos (2757m.), at the E end Peña de Otal (2705m.). The highest point is the Tendeñera. This ridge is rarely visited; its eastern end is seen when descending to Spain from the Port de Gavarnie.

From Bujaruelo. This hamlet (1338m.) is reached from Gavarnie by the road to the Port de Gavarnie and the rough road (new toll road under construction) leading down to the Ara valley. About one km. before the hamlet, a track cuts back R (W) into the broad Otal valley rising to the Collada de Tendeñera (2250m.) at the top. This track cuts across a tractor road rising in long zigzags in the same direction that starts further back (NW) from the Ara road. Follow a path eventually on R side of the stream, gradually climbing away on the N side of the valley to reach the col, 6.5km. from the Ara valley. From here the summit lies almost due S. Find a faint track heading SW which leads with an abrupt slope to finish on the main ridge just W of the summit. 4-5h. from Bujaruelo.

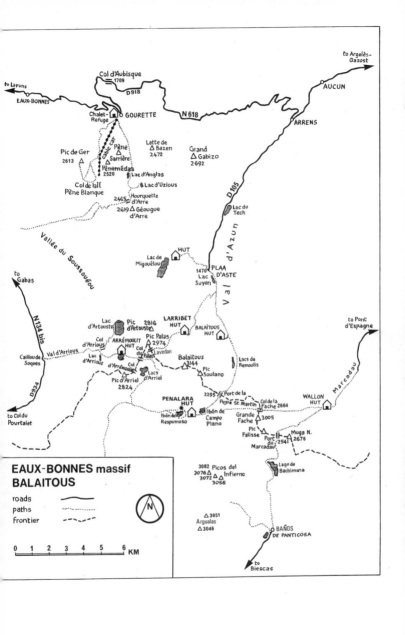

Eaux - Bonnes Massif

Maps: IGN 50m. n.1647. IGN/RP 50m. n.3. IGN 25m.V n.274.

This limestone massif lies to the S of the western half of the Laruns to Argelès-Gazost road. Its summits are modest in height, between 2500-2600m. The most convenient base is Gourette, a skiing centre 14km. from Laruns. A broad valley rises to the S of Gourette, bounded on the W by the Ger ridge and on the E by another ridge with the Latte de Bazen. In the centre of the valley, dividing its upper slopes, is a shorter ridge, the Pènemédaa. The head of the valley is closed by the Pène-Blanque ridge. To the SE of the Latte de Bazen are the Grand and Petit Gabizos. The area contains a handful of high lakes, paths for mountain walks and climbs of all grades.

PIC DE GER 2613m.

Traverse: Col des Coutchets to Col d'Amoulat.
Grade, PD. Because Gourette is a fast expanding ski resort, the lower slopes of the valley are cut up by broad bull-dozed pistes which rapidly multiply year by year. This makes accurate description of the start of routes impossible. The main cableway from the village to the head of the valley provides a stable point of reference.

From the village go up to the cableway station, pass under the cable and turn L up a broad piste. When this bears L, leave it and continue S over rough scrub. Another piste is met at R-angles; turn R and follow it. A building (café during the winter season) is seen a little to the R. On drawing level with it, turn L on a path which gradually converges on the cable line. Follow under it to the mid-way station (1768m.). Here the Pènemédaa ridge is close at hand to the L and the Ger ridge across the valley to the R. This ridge curves round NE and falls to a saddle, Col des Coutchets, before rising to a final sharp peak, Pic des Coutchets.

At the mid-way station drop down the valley then climb grass slopes W (no path) to the Col des Coutchets (2226m.). Now turn SW up the ridge, keeping on the R flank over moderately sloping slabs conveniently riven by a large number of cracks broad enough to stand in comfortably; stay below the crest. As the ridge nears its junction with the main Ger ridge at a secondary summit, Turon de Ger (2533m.), the cracks become less helpful, the slabs steeper and care must be taken.

From the Turon, go S along the main ridge crest. After a few m. this becomes too narrow to walk on and there are no good holds on either of the very steep sides. It is best taken sitting astride the crest and levering oneself along. This passage is short; rope advised for the less experienced. The ridge then widens a little and can be followed without difficulty, rising slightly to the next top, Salon de Ger (2611m.). The highest point lies a little further along the ridge, beyond a gap (2580m.). Follow down the crest with a sharp drop, again very narrow, then go up easily to the Pic de Ger. 3-4h. from Gourette.

The descent which follows is the easy normal ascent route. From summit a path with yellow-green markings drops down the W flank of the S ridge, getting well below the crest until it rejoins it and cuts through at the Col d'Amoulat (2445m.) under a rock hillock (2496m.). Now the yellow green path skirts E, round below the slopes of Pic d'Amoulat, then goes on beneath the head of the valley as far as the upper cableway station under the Pène-Blanque. From this path, a little below the col, another path, marked red, drops down scree slopes into the valley and leads to the mid-way station. In summer the cableway starts at 09.30. Much time can be saved by using it.

Mountain walk.
By the Col de la Pène-Blanque, Hourquette d'Arre and the Lac d'Anglas; a circular tour from, and returning to, Gourette. Take the cablecar to the upper station (2376m.), or walk. Pass behind the terminus on a yellow green marked path SW which reaches the Col de la Pène-Blanque in about 20 min. (2420m.). Fine view to S and SW, including the Balaitous, Pic Palas and Pic d'Ossau.

No path on S side of col, so descend obliquely R, an easy scramble down rocks. A small tarn (2234m.) is seen below. Make a line for it from the foot of the escarpment. This place is called Clot des Espagnols; the word 'clot' means hollow. The connection with Spaniards suggests that they formerly had grazing rights here as at many places on the French side of the frontier.

Follow the L bank of the stream flowing from the tarn, bearing round SE; grass slopes and irises. In a hollow (pt.1978m.) the waymarked GR 10 path is met coming up from the Soussouéou valley. Turn L (NE) up this track, leading towards abandoned mine workings. Before reaching them, it turns S - not very distinct - and near pt.2091 turns E to start a long climb to the Hourquette d'Arre, with the slopes of the Géougue d'Arre (2619m.) rising to the R of the track. Reach the Arre col (2465m.) and bear L (NE). The path drops gently and soon passes a hut R of the track; PNP signpost. The path winds down N, veers E and again N, and descends in a series of zigzags to the Lac d'Anglas (2068m.). Go along E shore of lake below old mine workings; at the N end cross grassy hillocks - path indistinct - to find the path on the L bank of the stream (falls) flowing from the lake. It goes into the Valentin valley, with the Latte de Bazen rising E and the vertical wall of the Pène Sarrière to the W. The path keeps to the L bank of the stream, then works further L and finishes by a ski piste leading down to Gourette. From the upper cableway station, back to Gourette, about 5h.

Gustav Doré impression (1867) of Pic de Ger.

Balaitous

Maps: IGN 50m. n.1647,1648. IGN/RP 50m. n.3 IGN 25m.V n. 274. EA 25m. n.203.

The most westerly of the 3000m. peaks, the Balaitous stands on the frontier S of the Eaux-Bonnes massif; to the W of the upper Val d' Azun and E of the Ossau valley. It is not visible from any motor road except, distantly, from the Col du Tourmalet. It lies in savage country. The massive central peak puts out long ridges in all directions. A number of small glaciers lie around the central peak, the largest being the Glacier de las Néous. Four huts round the mountain provide access to a variety of routes.

Refuge d'Arrémoulit 2304m.

The usual route starts from Caillou de Soques in the upper Ossau valley (see Ossau section). From the mound serving as a carpark, go past an old hut built against a huge boulder, turn L round it and cross a stream to join the good HRP path rising E. It passes through woods and emerges in the pastures of the Val d'Arrious. Follow the clear path up the valley, passing a cheese-maker's hut to the R of the path. At the head of the valley, Col d'Arrious (2259m.), signpost; turn sharp R on a lesser path leading after 200m. to the narrow Lac d'Arrious. The path rises on the E bank of the lake, crosses a low crest, then becomes a narrow, curving ledge with a high rock wall R and a very steep slope L; the Passage d'Orteig. The large Lac d'Artouste is seen below to the N. At the end of the "passage", the path crosses some smooth rocks (cairns) and the hut appears below on the N side of the larger of the Arrémoulit lakes. 3-3½h. from Caillou de Soques.

Refuge de Larribet 2070m.

From Arrens village on the Laruns to Argelès-Gazost road, a road now D.105 runs SSW up the Val d'Azun, past the Tech dam and lake, to end at Plaa d'Aste, 11km. from Arrens. Large carpark, PNP Reception Centre and museum (1470m.). From the carpark, cross the stream by a bridge. The broad track turns S through woods, then into the open valley with the Lac de Suyen ahead. About 250m. beyond the lake leave the main track up the valley, and fork R. Cross the stream by a shepherd's hut. On the other side is a huge boulder with a hollow under it. This is the Toue de Doumblas; it was in such places as this that Henry Russell frequently passed his nights.

The path rises W and, passing through a zone of firs and boulders, reaches a flat valley of lawns and clear shallow streams of unusual beauty. Continue, crossing the streams several times, then cross a rocky but low ridge to the S. Bear R and follow the path to the hut, seen a little above to the R. It is built on the site of the base camp established by Peytier and Hossard of the military survey team who first climbed Balaitous. Plaque on wall of hut. The mountain is seen 2km. away to the S. From Plaa d'Aste, $2\frac{1}{2}$ h.

Refuge du Balaitous (Ledormeur) 1917m.

This hut, lacking in all amenities, is now seldom used. Follow the way to the Larribet hut past the Suyen lake to the fork. Continue L on the main track for about 2km. At this point look for a footbridge across the stream to R of the path. Cross bridge and find a path climbing the western side of the valley which, turning N, soon reaches the hut. About 2 h. from Plaa d'Aste.

Refugio Peñalara (Piedrafita) 2140m.

See also introductory section on huts. From Plaa d'Aste the main track up the Val d'Azun (see above) is taken; continue at length, past the Remoulis lakes (5km.) to the frontier at the Port de la Peyre St.Martin (2295m.); frontier stone n.312 (7.5km. from Plaa d'Aste). On the Sp. side go down SW to the Campo Plano lake in one km., then along its S side and follow a path W via small tarns to near the old hut. Bear R (NW) along a track crossing infall beds, round to the new hut on N side of the Respumoso reservoir. About $5\frac{1}{2}$ h. from Plaa d'Aste.

Arrémoulit - Larribet huts connection
by the Port du Lavedan 2615m.

Grade, F+. This excursion of something under 5km. and part of the HRP will take longer than expected; it is for seasoned walkers only. Arrémoulit hut to Col du Palas (2517m.), as for the Balaitous normal route, below. At the col go sharp L on a path falling gradually to skirt below the ends of 2 spurs coming down from the Palas SW ridge. Path faint at times and patches of sliding scree. After rounding the second spur the path disappears and the line is marked by small cairns. The Port du Lavedan saddle is seen in the Palas SE ridge. Early in July a long stretch of snow below the saddle is likely; this may make the crossing delicate (crampons for safety); ask the hut keeper about the conditions before leaving. The are 2 passages on the saddle. The L-hand one is easier to reach but leads to very steep gullies with some loose rock on the other (French) side. The R-hand is reached by a short, steep but easy gully, and it leads to a path; this route is preferable. The path drops down to the Batcrabère valley and usually

64

crosses extensive snow patches before reaching a more distinct path near the Micoulaou tarns. It passes E of the upper Batcrabère lake then goes up a little to the Br. de la Garénère (2189m.) from where it descends to the Larribet hut. 5–6h. depending on conditions at the Port du Lavedan.

BALAITOUS 3144m.

Sp. Balaitus. IGC 3151m. The normal Spanish route joins the French one in the Arriel cwm. It starts from Sallent de Gallego (1305m.) and takes the valley road N via the Sarra reservoir (roadhead), the continuation track then the path as for the Peñalara hut, as far as the Onso flats (1700m.) where the main valley heads E. A path climbs N into the Arriel cwm and joins the French approach near the Gourg Glacé, 2½h. from roadhead. Thence to the summit in a further 3h. or less. The easiest route from the Peñalara hut goes NNE up the Respumoso barranco, followed by a steep rough ascent W to the Br. Latour (2945m.) in the S ridge, which is taken up across a snowy roof-like rock slope to the summit. PD, 4h.

Normal Route.
Grade, F. From the Arrémoulit hut, situated under the W face of Pic Palas, a ridge will be seen falling SW from this summit. There are 2 passes in this ridge; the Col du Palas, under a sharp drop in the skyline of the ridge, and the Col d'Arrémoulit further SW. While either of these passes can be taken, the Palas one is preferable as less height is lost on the way beyond the ridge. Leave the hut and pass above the NE side of the lake on a line a little S of E. Rise over rocky ground where until late summer there is usually a longish stretch of snow to the Col du Palas (2517m.), one km. from the hut.

On the Spanish side there are 2 paths. One, sharp L, leads to the Port de Lavedan (see above); the other begins to drop half L round the cirque above the Arriel lakes seen below but, curving to pass above the E bank of the inner lake, does not reach them. Follow the latter, crossing a snow patch before reaching the E side of the bowl. The path runs S until a kind of gully of loose reddish grit is reached. Cross this and climb to a narrow rocky gap through which the stream falls (2404m.). Go through the gap and continue on the N side of a half-frozen tarn, the Gourg Glacé. Ahead lies a slope of chaotic boulders. Bear a little L away from the stream flowing into the tarn. Scramble rocks and snow patches to the L of a bluff (2644m.) and, more steeply, to a point where the W wall of the Balaitous falls to the jumble of rocks. Here will be found a natural shelter, improved by a wall of stones and a door; Abri Michaud (2698m.). About 3h. from hut.

Climb L from the shelter over boulders to a gully which marks the start

of the ascent proper. The gully is easy, with a near vertical wall R.
At the top the track moves out L on to an unexpected grass platform.
Here is the frontier ridge. To the N a needle (Aig. Lamathe) is seen
on the NW ridge, and also visible an apparently steep ledge rising
diagonally across the NW face of the mountain. This is the Grande
Diagonale and our route. Turn R and reach the foot of this ledge; it
is wider than expected and less steep. Climb it on broken rocks to
about 150m. from its head, marked by a gendarme to the L of the ledge.
A cairn indicates the place where you must leave the Diagonale by
climbing a wall R by a short easy gully. This leads to the broad roof
of the Balaitous; walk to the summit cairn. $4\frac{1}{2}$-5h. from hut. In
descent, 3-$3\frac{1}{2}$h.

The view is very extensive. To the SE is seen the pyramid of the Gde.
Fache and, beyond, Vignemale. To the NW is the Palas; the Pic d'
Ossau lies to the W. To the N are summits of the Eaux-Bonnes massif.

From North.
Above the Larribet hut the broad Pabat valley suggests an easy route
to the Balaitous whose summit is seen at its head. In fact, all approaches from the N are far from simple, owing to the complicated topo-
graphy of the ground on this side. The following route is the easiest
and offers alternative finishes. The approach is tedious.

To Brèche Peytier-Hossard. From the Larribet hut take the
path leading down from the hut for a short way, then turn R and start
ascending boulder slopes to pass L of a curving escarpment and reach
a point E of pt.2062. Continue up steep, laborious slopes under the
Fachon crest to your L and climb S to the Col du Pabat (2598m.). On
the other side of this pass bear R (S), traversing a steep slope of boulders and snow above the little Lac des Tuts (2504m.), and contour a
shoulder to reach the Néous glacier. Go up the R side of this narrowing snow slope and, near its head, move R to the Peytier-Hossard gap
(2989m.) under the NE summit ridge, running out R in the near horizontal promontory of Cap Peytier-Hossard (2995m.). $3\frac{1}{2}$-4h. from hut.

Vire Béraldi finish. Grade, PD-. Cross the gap; on the other
side (N) this vire (ledge) will be seen rising W across the N wall of
the mountain. It is short but cut by 2 gullies which may be choked by
snow; if so, they will require proper safety techniques with rope, etc.
If the gullies are clear there is no difficulty. The ledge leads round L
to the top of the Grande Diagonale of the normal route, with a gendarme, actually the head of a buttress, to your R. This place, prominent from a distance, is called the Br. des Isards. Go down the Diagonale to the cairn marking the gully on the L, leading to the summit,
as for the normal route. About 1h. from the Peytier-Hossard gap.

Balaitous. W face seen from Pic Palas.

Néous Chimney finish. Grade, AD-. Coming up the glacier, there is no need to go to the gap on R. On approaching it, head up the glacier to the foot of the second chimney in the Balaitous face, counting from the gap. Crevasses, bergschrund, steep snow/ice pitch possible Rope necessary. The lower part of the chimney is the more difficult and will probably have wet and slippery rock. The first short pitch ends under an overhang which is turned R. The next has rather poor holds but is short and ends at a broad ledge. After another short easier pitch the chimney broadens into a fairly wide gully, which is climbed without difficulty to the summit. About 1h. from the glacier.

Henry Russell has a splendid description of this route, which he climbed in 1870, ending with: Hardly out of the chimney, one suddenly sees, a few paces to the left, the highest point of the formidable Balaitous ... I was half-mad with joy to see the cairn: This was the first ascent by this chimney.

Note on rock climbs

The main routes are on the ridges. The Costerillou ridge runs E from the summit then curves S to Pic Sulano (2911m.). Studded with towers and needles, traverses in either direction are graded, D. S of the Sulano, the ridge continues as the Crête du Diable, an even fiercer crest with points picturesquely named the N and S Trident, Devil's Horns, Pte. Lucifer, and Devil's Dog-tooth. Again, traverses in either direction are D, sometimes with pitches of V. These ridges are most conveniently reached from the Peñalara hut.

PIC PALAS 2974m.

An attractively shaped pyramid, standing 2km. NE of the Balaitous. It was first climbed by accident. When, in 1825, Peytier and Hossard of the army survey unit were looking for the Balaitous, from which they wanted to take sightings, they climbed the Palas believing they were on the Balaitous. They discovered their error on reaching the summit.

North Ridge. Normal route, grade PD-. From the Arrémoulit hut take the route towards the Col du Palas (Balaitous normal route, above). About halfway to the pass, turn L (NE), climb slopes of boulders then curve round gradually, clockwise, to cross below the foot of the Palas W ridge and that of the NNW ridge near shoulder pt.2616, rising steadily to reach the N ridge between the Palas and Pic d'Artouste to the N, at the Br. des Géodésiens (2786m.). Ascend the ridge (boulders) and after a short narrow section reach the foot of a much steeper part. Turn this by passing to a ledge on the R (W) side. This rises obliquely to rejoin the ridge crest once more. Follow crest over large boulders to summit. 3½h. from hut. Outstanding view SE of the Balaitous.

PIC D'ARRIEL 2824m.

An obvious peak across the lake S of the Arrémoulit hut. The E ridge defines the L skyline. It drops steeply then rises to a minor pt. 2697m. To the R of a depression thus formed, a diagonal gully is seen falling from L to R to snow slopes beneath the ridge (small glacier). This gully marks the route to be taken to reach the ridge. If it is seen to be filled with snow in mid season the climb should not be tried, as it is prone to avalanche conditions, altogether variable according to season. It may be bare in one August and deep soft snow in another.

Diagonal Gully and East Ridge. Grade, PD. From the hut cross the stream flowing from the lake and turn L along the W bank, rising by easy rocks to slopes of grit then snow. Trend R and climb obliquely, making for a point immediately below the summit. A small bergschrund may be found here. Turn L under the face and follow it round on steep snow to the foot of the diagonal gully. Ascend to foot of gully by a spur of rock. Climb the gully over loose boulders, keeping to the R for preference, and reach the ridge. This is followed with no difficulty to the summit. $3-3\frac{1}{2}$ h. from hut.

The descent may be made by a slightly easier route, also technically the easiest way up the mountain. Go down the easy NW ridge to the Col d'Arriel (2608m.). Now descend a gully of boulders and/or snow to reach the slopes above the lakes where the outward approach is joined. About 2 h. from summit to hut.

Marcadau

Maps: IGN 50m. n.1647, 1648. IGN/RP 50m. n.3. IGN 25m. V n.274. EA 25m. n.203.

A comparatively small district to the SW of Cauterets, but one of exceptional charm. It contains none of the greater peaks, though among the ring of mountains round the head of the Marcadau valley, the Gde. Fache reaches the 3000m. mark. Good mountain walking country with opportunities for interesting excursions into Spain. There is one hut in the area from which most routes start.

Refuge Wallon 1865m.

A road runs up from Cauterets to Pont d'Espagne (1496m.), at the entrance to the Marcadau valley. Large carpark just below the bridge, from which the path to the Lac de Gaube leaves. Further on the road re-crosses the stream, deteriorates for cars, and ends 3km. beyond the Pont du Cayan (1630m.). For those who prefer it, there is a pleasant walk on a near-level path on the opposite (R) side of the stream, leaving the road a little before it crosses to the L side.

From the Cayan bridge a good path winds up through woods, moving a little away from the stream, then, without rising, joins it again at the Pont d'Estalounqué (1.2km. from Cayan bridge). Cross the bridge and follow R side along a delightful reach of the very clear stream. The path rises over rocky ground among Scotch pines and, about 2km. from the last bridge, attains pastures where the entrance to the Aratille valley is seen to the SE. The path turns R and reaches the hut. About $1\frac{1}{4}$h. from Cayan bridge. Pleasant chapel nearby.

GRANDE FACHE 3005m.

Sp. Gran Faxa (Pico da Faxa). A rust coloured pyramid seen to the W from the Wallon hut. At sunrise it glows like copper. A pleasant approach walk and an easy scramble.

Normal Route. Grade, F. From the hut descend SW and cross a bridge. Turn R along the stream and after 500m. re-cross it by a second bridge. Turn L, then the path forks. Take the track ascending first by zigzags over grass slopes heading W, all much improved lately. After about one km. the natural route appears to pass between the two points marked 2360 and 2341; however, skirt S of pt.2360 and pass above a tarn on your R. The path continues W by slopes sometimes snow covered to reach the Col de la Fache (2664m.) on a N-S section of the frontier. Fine view of the Balaitous and the Frondella ridges to the S of it; also from here a rough path leads straight down past the Fache lakes to the Campo Plano lake, just visible, and the Peñalara hut.

The Gde. Fache N ridge rises from the col. Turn up the ridge by a plain path that keeps a little below the crest on the W side. This path is so well worn that it can hardly be lost. It winds up by easy steps and reaches the crest a little below the summit. Follow crest to the cairn. $3\frac{1}{2}$ h. from hut.

The view of the Balaitous is splendid. The Pic d'Ossau is seen to the L of the Frondella ridges. To the SW is the ridge summit of the Picos del Infierno, divided by buttresses on their NE face into 3 steep slopes of snow. To the SE is the Vignemale.

Mountain walk to Baños de Panticosa
by the Port du Marcadau

Start as for the Gde. Fache. At the second bridge, take the path fork SW, along near the R side of the stream, to follow up a spur dividing the valley bed, then mounting by zigzags. So cross the Marcadau bed twice and go up through an area of boulders past a spring, Hount Frido (Cold Spring). Finally ascend stony slopes SSW to the Port du Marcadau (2541m., frontier stone n.313) between the Muga (E) and Pic Falisse (NW). The Picos del Infierno are seen to the SW, and to the S is the long flat line of the Sierra Tendeñera.

From the pass the path falls by short zigzags (snow patches) to the W end of the smaller Pecico lake, and after running along its N side, it drops S over rock terraces for a little over one km., when it approaches the large Bachimaña lake. The path takes a wide sweep to the R and passes round, but not close to, the N and W sides of the lake, reaching it again near the dam at its S end. The path now descends in zigzags (waterfall to L), and follows the R bank of the stream through a gorge. At the lower end of this turn L over a footbridge and drop down to the Panticosa Baths a few min. away. Apart from the Baths there are large hotels, a few shops and a useful bank for currency exchange. About 5h. from the Wallon hut. See also entry below.

PICOS DEL INFIERNO IGC 3082m. IGN 3076m.

PICOS DE LAS ARGUALAS 3051m.

A conspicuous massif in Spain, 8km. SSE of the Balaitous and 4km. SSW of the Grande Fache, occupying the area between Sallent de Gallego (W) and Baños de Panticosa (E). Each of the 2 ridge sectors has multiple summits of much the same height, and sometimes with individual names. The NE side of the Infierno is frequently snow covered to late season. There are no huts in the massif. The best approach from the Peñalara hut to the N is over the Piedrafita saddle (2782m.) to the adjoining Infierno saddle (2721m.) at the foot of the Infierno N/NW ridge; 4h. to latter's summit. The usual routes start from the Panticosa Baths (1660m.), a rather posh watering place with some modest accommodation and a large inn owned by a local mountain association. The Pondiellos pass (2809m.), NW of the resort, is attained by a reasonable path in 3¼ h. It lies midway between the 2 ridge sectors, from where either is reached SW (Argualas) or NW (Infierno) in another 1½ h. or less. All mapping of this zone is deficient in matters of detail.

Picos del Infierno NE face, seen from the Grande Fache.

Vignemale

Maps: IGN 50m. n.1647, 1648. IGN/RP 50m. n.3, 4. IGN 25m. V n.274, 275. EA 40m. n.204.

The Vignemale is one of the great peaks of the Pyrenees by reason of its height, its great N face and its main glacier – the only one in the Pyrenees that makes any pretence to conform to the generally accepted idea of what a glacier should be. Even so, it is very modest by Alpine standards.

Standing on the frontier due S of Cauterets, it consists of a horseshoe of summits, all above 3200m. with the open end facing E. The closed end holds the feed basin of the Ossoue glacier. At the NW corner rises the highest point, Pique Longue, whose N face offers rock climbs of great length and severity. The W and SW faces rise in great butt-resses from the Ara valley in Spain.

The mountain is served by 2 huts as detailed below.

Refuge des Oulétes de Gaube   2151m.

From Pont d'Espagne (see Marcadau section), below the bridge, a path (GR 10 var.) ascends S through woods to the entrance of the Gaube valley. On leaving the woods the Vignemale N face is seen 7km. away at the top. A little under 2km. from Pont d'Espagne the path reaches the Lac de Gaube inn on the N bank of the lake; crowded with tourists in high season. (At Pont d'Espagne, a little beyond the hotel, a chair lift can be taken to a point from where a good horizontal path leads in 1.2km. to the lake).

Shortly before reaching the inn, branch R on a path skirting the end of the lake, cross a bridge and follow the good path along W side of the lake. At the S end the path crosses the infall stream by a bridge and starts to rise along the L side, to which it keeps for about 2km. It then re-crosses it. Now, impossible to lose the path up the valley, it mounts in easy stages to the hut. $3\frac{1}{2}$ h., or by using the chairlift, save 30 min.

Refuge de Bayssellance   2651m.

From Pont d'Espagne to the Gaube hut, as above. The path (GR 10) continues SE, slanting above a plateau resembling the bed of a lake, cut by several streams. It soon starts to rise in zigzags on the E slopes of the valley. As you approach the Hourquette d'Ossoue (2734m.) the view of the N face becomes more and more imposing. At the pass the

Bayssellance hut, shaped like a large black Nissen hut, can be seen about 600m. away down the eastern slope. About 6h. from the Espagne bridge.

From Gavarnie, take the road leading to the Port de Boucharo. After one km. this road bends back L at pt.1389; however, continue straight on up the Ossoue valley, in which the little road is good for 4km. Then come 4km. of very rough road which ends at the small Ossoue dam (1834m.) where cars can be left. A path (GR 10, HRP) continues up the valley, past the lake, with the stream on your L. After one km. on level grass it crosses the stream (bridge) and ascends above the L side; snow patches. It bears round R above a gorge then drops to the level of the stream, flowing from beneath snow. Bear R across the snow then join a path mounting again, northwards. The path is obvious and cannot be lost; after a further short drop it rises in many zigzags and passes in front of Henry Russell's 3 caves, the Grottes de Bellevue. From here the snout of the glacier can be seen. The hut is reached about one km. above the grottoes, but as it stands above the path to its R it cannot easily be seen until one has just passed it; several short tracks lead up to it. 3¾h. from Ossoue dam.

If the Gavarnie approach is used to reach the Gaube hut, allow 1½h. to go from the Bayssellance hut to Gaube hut.

GRAND VIGNEMALE : PIQUE LONGUE 3298m.

A simple walk up the glacier to its head followed by a short easy scramble on the final rock peak. Descriptions of this glacier from the last century show that it must have been a rather different proposition 100 years ago. Several people managed to fall into the Grande Crevasse, which then ran across its width. In normal summers all crevasses, and there are many, are safely covered by snow, over which there will be a well-beaten track to the foot of Pique Longue.

Ossoue Glacier Normal Route.

Grade, F. From the Bayssellance hut go down the Gavarnie path to a little above the Bellevue grottoes where, at a bend (2550m.), a narrow path leads off W towards the glacier, and runs horizontally across a steep slope of grit and scree. At the end the path descends half L to the rather untidy ground under the glacier snout. Turn L on a track, usually snow, passing S under the NE end of the glacier. This short section is subject to intermittent rock/ice falls. Reach smooth rocks and cairns; cross them, turn R and climb onto the glacier. As the snout varies according to season, it is not possible to indicate the precise spot where it should be boarded, but tracks in the snow should mark the way; sometimes there is a little bare ice. The track trends R and passes near a short open crevasse under the Petit Vignemale; go straight up the glacier. The gradient eases gradually and reaches the all but level upper basin, where the several peaks of the mountain can be seen. To the N, Pte. Chausenque (3204m.); to the NW, Pique Longue, separated from the Chausenque by a saddle (3152m.) which marks the exit of the Gaube Couloir on the N face. A little to the L of Pique Longue is the Pic du Clot de la Hount (3289m.); to the W, Pic de Cerbillona (3247m.) and Pic Central (3235m.). To the S is Montferrat (3219m.). All but Pique Longue rise only a short distance above the level of the glacier head.

From the upper basin bear half R to the foot of rocks and climb to the top – various ways – none marked – all equally easy. Russell's last and highest cave, the Paradis, will be seen a little below the summit. 2¾h. from hut. The view is pleasing. All the main peaks described in this guide can be seen; also, to the E, beyond Monte Perdido, the Posets (Pyrenees Central guide).

Note: Late in the season, or in mid season after a winter with light snowfall, crevasses can be open. Then the glacier needs care and rope work. Always ask the hut keeper about the state of the glacier. If the route is advised as "closed", an alternative lies in crossing below the whole width of the glacier and reaching the ridge falling E from Montferrat. Follow up the ridge on the glacier side of the crest, until a point is reached level with the upper basin, which is always safely snow covered. Go down on to the glacier and cross it to the foot of the Pique Longue rocks.

POINTE DE CHAUSENQUE   3204m.

This route includes the traverse of a very narrow but short descending ridge high above the Ossoue glacier to the S and the Petit Vignemale glacier to the N. Rope necessary.

By Petit Vignemale-Chausenque Ridge. Grade, AD-. Reach the Hourquette d'Ossoue from either the Gaube or Bayssellance huts (see above). From this pass take a path to the S, a well-worn track winding up boulders and grit on the ridge crest that rises to the Petit Vignemale (3032m.), 1h. from pass. The view of the Pique Longue N face and the séracs of the little Petit Vignemale glacier below is impressive. From the P.V. summit the greater part of the ridge to be taken from this point falls out of sight to the Col des Glaciers (2990m.). The route from this col, a broad crest rising to pt.3138m., is visible and appears excessively steep but this is an illusion.

Rope up, move L (S) on rocks and go down a very short gully. Turn L up to the start of the ridge. Keep on the N side, footholds, with hand

Vignemale N face and the Gaube hut. L to R: Chausenque, Gaube couloir, Pique Longue.

holds on the crest itself for a few m. Rise to the top of the ridge and
follow it to a point where there is a short near-vertical pitch down on
the S side. Below this pitch the ridge is followed to a second, rather
longer pitch down on the S side (III). Follow the ridge to the next
pitch down on the N side (III). Continue along the ridge with footholds on the N side, handholds on the crest, then descend by ledges
to the Col des Glaciers.

From here climb the slope to pt.3138, keeping to S side of the crest.
From pt.3138 go along crest to summit of the Chausenque. About 2h.
from Petit Vignemale. The easiest way to return is by dropping down
from the Chausenque to the Ossoue glacier, not many m. below, and
by taking the normal route down the glacier.

North Face
Looking at the skyline from the Gaube hut, on the L is the Petit Vignemale, followed R by the depression of the Col des Glaciers above
the P.V. glacier. Beyond, rises the Chausenque, and in front of this
section is the large triangular buttress of the Aig. des Glaciers. Now
R again the skyline drops to a notch above a deep gully, rises to the
irregular Piton Carré and falls to a deeper notch, marking the head of
the Gaube Couloir. Further R is the sharp peak of Pique Longue and
lastly the high Gaube ridge. The Gaube Couloir and the gully to the
R of the Chausenque join about halfway down the face; below are the
remnants of the Oulétes glacier.

On the N face there are no routes graded below D. Many are TD or
ED. Mention has been made in the introductory historical notes of the
first ascent of the Gaube Couloir in 1889, but it was not until the late
1930s that routes began to be worked out on the face of Pique Longue.
This rockface is about 800m. high and all routes on it are exposed
throughout. It was not until 1967 that a "direct" to Pique Longue was
achieved. Routes on the Chausenque N face, only a little shorter, are
of equal severity.

West and South-West Faces.
These are relatively seldom seen
by visitors. They stand above the head of the Ara valley in Spain, a
region reached, with one exception, by long approach marches. The
exception is described below.

Gaube hut to Upper Ara valley.
From the hut follow a path S (not GR 10), then keep R across the plain
cut by streams where a path starts to climb W up a steep slope to the
Col des Mulets (2591m.), about one km. from the foot of the slope. The
head of the Ara valley lies below; descend W into it, reach the main
stream and follow it S down on the L bank. The buttressed mass of the

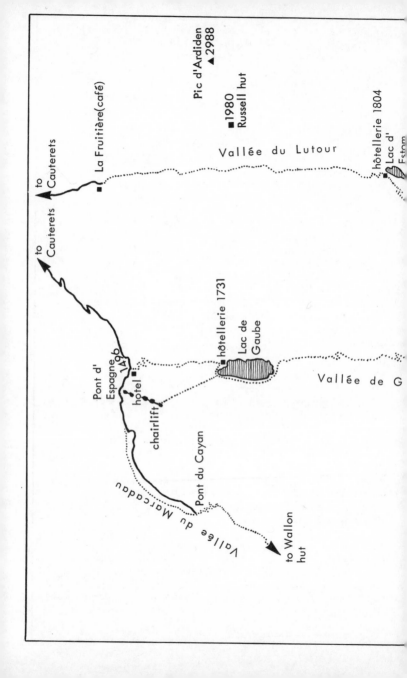

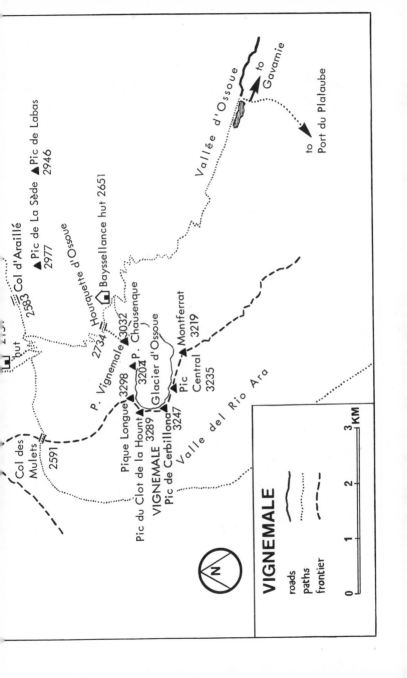

Pic du Clot de la Hount and the Pic de Cerbillona rises to the E. Ways up the great gullies between the buttresses are not of great difficulty, but are laborious. The Ara river is crossed to the R side by a footbridge below a shepherd's hut after 2.5km., returning to the L side a little lower down. S of this point the valley turns SE below the Pic Central and Montferrat. If it is intended to climb the historic Prince de la Moskowa's Route, it is advisable to camp in the Ara valley as near to the start of the route as possible. Therefore the L side of the Ara is followed down from the footbridge for 2km. to a second shepherd's hut standing above the path (1827m.). An ideal bivvy spot is halfway along this stretch, beside the Labaza torrent. About 4h. from Gaube hut.

Prince de la Moskowa's Route.

Grade, AD-. Climbed by Miss Lister and the Prince de la Moskowa in August 1838. It may be thought odd that the first tourist ascents were made by a relatively difficult route. Cazaux and Guillembet made the first ascent in 1835 by the Ossoue glacier but on the way up they fell into a crevasse — or so Cazaux claimed — but were able to climb out of it and reach the summit of Pique Longue. Because of their mishap on the glacier, they sought another way down and found this descent into the Ara valley.

From the shepherd's hut (1827m.) in the Ara valley, go back along the level path for one km. to the Labaza torrent. Climb slopes NE on the L side of this, leading wearily to a high small cirque under the S face of the Cerbillona-Central-Montferrat. In the cirque (c.2700m.) bear L towards the foot of a steep gully (well drawn on map), the upper half snow-filled, which lies between a ridge L falling S from Cerbillona and a ridge R coming off Pic Central. Work up this gully; after narrowing it widens again towards steeper headslopes. As it widens, bear L to rocks of the Cerbillona ridge at the foot of a 50m. chimney of rather poor rock (II). Climb the chimney (III, rope advisable) and reach the ridge. Follow the ridge, but before attaining its top leave it and traverse R onto a slope of boulders that leads up to a shallow saddle between Cerbillona and Pic Central ("Col Lady Lyster", sic,IGN 3200m.). This is a few m. above the flat upper basin of the Ossoue glacier. Pique Longue is seen N across the glacier, about 400m. away. From Ara valley to Ossoue glacier, 3-4h.

This route can also be reached from the Ossoue valley by crossing into the Ara valley by the Port de Plalaube - long, and camping/open biv. almost essential.

Mountain walk.

Lutour valley, Col d'Araillé and Gaube valley.

On the road from Cauterets to Pont d'Espagne, about one km. above the baths of La Raillère, a road branches L by a sharp backward bend E (1134m.), then turns S into the Lutour valley; this runs due S and parallel to the Gaube valley to the W. The branch road ends after 2.5km. at a café, La Fruitière.

From here cross the stream to its L side and follow the path along it for a little over 3km. when a bridge (1552m.) is reached, taking the path to the R side. The valley is very beautiful, very green and has a fine backdrop to the S in the massive Pic de Labas (2946m.). The R side of the stream is followed to the little Lac d'Estom at the head of the valley, where a refuge/inn is found (1804m.).

From here the path rises SW across the W flank of the valley towards the Col d'Araillé, moderately at first then in 2 sets of zigzags, higher up possibly with snow patches, and latterly in boulders to the saddle (2583m.). The Vignemale N face appears to the SW. The path descends the E slope of the Gaube valley and soon joins the path coming down from the Hourquette d'Ossoue. Follow this in zigzags W and NW, down past the Gaube hut and onwards N to the Pont d'Espagne. (See route from Pont d'Espagne to Gaube hut and Bayssellance hut, above). 5–6h. from La Fruitière to Pont d'Espagne.

PIC D'ARDIDEN   2988m.

This summit lies between the Lutour valley and the valley of the Gave de Pau. A long, rough promenade to a prominent landmark.

Normal Route. Grade, F. From the roadhead at La Fruitière in the Latour valley (carpark) cross the bridge and follow the path up the valley on the E side of the river for 3km., to where a path branches L (1537m., signpost) and climbs in zigzags (called the Sentier Falisse) to the Refuge Russell (1980m.); no amenities here. From this old TCF hut bear SE on a path leading to the Col de Culaus, and after about 500m. turn NE on a faint track, some cairns, through a field of boulders. The track bears N towards an obvious saddle, the Pourtau des Agudes, in the W ridge of the Ardiden. Climb to the saddle (2566m.), cross it and bear R to follow the ridge of loose, broken boulders to the summit. 4–5h. from La Fruitière. It is advisable to avoid passing the night at the Russell hut by making an early start from La Fruitière.

Brèche de Roland and its hut, seen from the N.

Gavarnie - Ordesa - Monte Perdido

Maps: IGN 50m. n.1648, 1748. IGN/RP 50m. n.4. IGN 25m.V
n.275. EA 40m. n.204

Introductory

Gavarnie village (1375m.) is the most visited place in the Pyrenees.
Each day throughout the season scores of coaches come up from Lourdes,
besides hundreds of cars. All the coaches and most of the cars go down
again each evening. The attraction is the famous Cirque de Gavarnie
and the Grande Cascade falling into it. It is traditional to cover the
4km. from the village to the cirque on horseback. Consequently Gavarnie stables a vast number of horses and during the day the village
street and the track to the cirque are never free from a fine permeating
manure dust. Those setting out by this track are strongly advised to
make an early start before the cavalcades begin to operate.

The Gavarnie cirque is a semi-circular bowl about one km. in diameter
at its base with the floor at c.1600m. The cliffs to the S rise in 3 horizontal walls, cut by 2 broad sloping ledges or terraces. The rim of the
upper wall is just under 3000m. and is crowned by 2 minor summits, the
Casque (3006m.) to the W, and the Tour (3009m.) in the centre. The
central and upper walls both extend W beyond the curve of the cirque,
the upper being the longer extension and cut towards its W end by the
famous Brèche de Roland (2807m.).

The the L (E) of the wall, in a curve NE, are, anti-clockwise, the 3
Pics de la Cascade (3095m, 3106m, 3161m.), then the massive Marboré
(3248m.), followed by the twin Astazou peaks (3012m, 3071m.) facing
Gavarnie village. To the W, beyond the Br. de Roland, is the pyramid of the Taillon (3144m.). Screening the Br. de Roland from the
village is the Sarradets ridge. The frontier runs from the Taillon through the Brèche, along the top of the upper wall of the cirque, then
curves NE through the Cascade tops and the Marboré to the Astazou,
where it turns E.

From the Marboré, a big spur thrusts to the SE with 3 peaks, Cilindro
(3325m.), Monte Perdido (3355m.) and the Sum de Ramond (3263m.).
S of the frontier the terrain slopes gradually to about 2400m. when it
is cut by the great Ordesa canyon, running roughly parallel to the Gavarnie walls.

The area has 6 huts: Refuge de la Brèche de Roland or des Sarradets,
below the Brèche; Refugio Delgado Ubeda and the old Goriz refuge

rather lower, beneath the S side of Monte Perdido; Refuge des Espuguettes on the Pailla pastures; and Refuge de Gavarnie and the Especières centre, both on the Gavarnie-Port de Gavarnie road (D.923).

Refuge de la Brèche de Roland   2587m.

Leave Gavarnie by the track leading S to the cirque. A few m. beyond the Hôtel du Cirque, take a path dropping R to cross the stream
by a footbridge. The path slants SW and ascends to the foot of the Echelle, a broad slope of well-worn rock steps mounting N. A little
higher it curves W, reaches grass slopes, then turns S to the foot of a
low rock wall. Magnificent view from here into the cirque and of the
Grande Cascade and the Marboré. Now the path ascends the steep
grass slopes of the Sarradets valley W again. It bears L to pass through a rock gap to reach the western extension of the very broad
upper terrace of the cirque. The hut is seen in the distance to the W.
The path moves up gradually over low rock terraces to the hut. To
the S is the Casque above the upper wall, to the N the Sarradets
ridge. 3½h. from Gavarnie.

Alternative way by the Tourettes (Pouey Aspé) valley. Leave Gavarnie by the path that starts from the church and gradually rises on the
W slope of the valley. After 2 short series of zigzags the path crosses
pasture and bears W on slopes above the N bank of the Tourettes stream, draining from the Port de Gavarnie. The very plain path, almost level, passes under cliffs and reaches a point level with the stream
where a signpost (1873m.) indicates the route for the hut. Fork L and
ascend S in long zigzags over grass slopes to reach a flat rocky area
where the path becomes rather indistinct. Cross this, bearing slightly
L, and pick up the path again, winding L close under the Sarradets
ridge. It now climbs between the Sarradets and the lower slopes of the
Taillon to the R, and goes up a lateral moraine to reach snow at the
foot of the covered Taillon glacier. A deep track SE in snow indicates the way up a fairly steep slope. A stream under the snow is visible
in places through holes. When the slope eases, the Col des Sarradets
is seen above to the L. Climb to its northern end (2589m.); from here
the hut is seen a few m. below its southern end about 250m. away.
3½h. from Gavarnie.

By the Port de Gavarnie road. Drive up the D.923 from Gavarnie to
the frontier; parking area on the pass (2270m.). From here a broad
new path runs roughly E across the lower slopes of the N face of the
Taillon. It barely rises and one km. further a noticeboard advises that
those not properly equipped should go no further - generally ignored
by those who should be concerned. The path continues, crossing snow
patches, and after a short sharp rise joins the track coming from the
Tourettes stream (see above), where this reaches the snow. Follow it

to the hut, about 1¾h. from Port de Gavarnie. Taxi hire to col, easy.

Walls of the Cirque de Gavarnie

As noted above, the S wall of the cirque is composed of 3 horizontal walls, one above the other, and separated by 2 broad sloping terraces. There are a large number of climbing routes on the walls; none of them is easy. The L side of the lowest wall, known as the Cascade Wall, not after the Grande Cascade which is further round to the L, but after a lesser fall at the L-hand side of the wall, has a classic route graded AD; but it is always wet and can be dangerous after a heavy thunderstorm. All other routes on the wall have a high grading.

There are also routes along the terraces. Those on the lower one are difficult but a route on the upper terrace, reached by the Echelle des Sarradets approach to the Brèche hut is only PD. The final part of this approach to the hut is in fact on the western extension of the upper terrace. The slope of this terrace beneath the Tour and above the cirque is considerable and care must be taken. Winter climbs on frozen falls and waterslides, which vary considerably from year to year, have been much in vogue during the 1970s. For a rock climb on the upper wall, see note below under the entry, Tour du Marboré.

PIMÉNÉ 2801m.

A minor but impressive limestone nappe E of Gavarnie. An easy and popular mountain walk made worthwhile by the very fine view from the summit not only of all the peaks of this region, including Monte Perdido, which is not seen from the Gavarnie valley, but also of the majority of the peaks W of the Garonne gap.

Normal Route. Ungraded. From the Gavarnie take the road to the cirque as far as the Pont de Nadau (1392m.), a stone humped bridge where the track crosses to the E side of the stream, one km. from the village. On the other side go back a little to where the path goes up E beside the largely dried-up bed of a stream. This climbs fairly steeply and, after passing isolated pines, reaches the Pailla pastures (PNP signpost). Continue towards a hut (1800m.). The path swings N and in a wide arc turns again to the SE (fine view of the twin Astazou summits to S). It continues to rise gently in broad sweeps over the pastures and reaches the PNP Espuguettes hut (2027m.). After this the path approaches an escarpment to the E and divides (2260m.). The R-hand fork leads to the Hourquette d'Alans. Take the L fork winding N in zigzags to the crest of the Piméné S ridge at pt.2522. Cross to the E side of the ridge and continue N under the crest. The path then rises over rocks to below the E side of the Petit Piméné (2667m.). It reaches the ridge further N at pt.2647 and the crest is duly followed to the summit. 4 h.

Monte Perdido, Casque, Brèche de Roland and Fausse Brèche from the NW.

LE TAILLON 3144m.

The easiest 3000m. summit in the Pyrenees and just a walk from the Br. Roland hut. As the route passes through the Brèche, a note about this curious gateway and its name may be of interest. It is about 100m. in height and 40m. wide, caused by the collapse of the frontier wall, very thin at this point. Its connection with Roland, Charlemagne's nephew, is purely imaginary. On 15 August, 778, Roland commanded Charlemagne's rearguard on a withdrawal of his forces from Spain by the Pass of Roncevaux, about 100km. W of Gavarnie. According to the ancient epic poem, the Song of Roland, the rearguard was attacked and overwhelmed by a strong force of "Saracens", ie. Moors. When all was lost and Roland mortally wounded, he tried to break his magical sword, Durandal, by striking it on a rock. The rock was split but the sword remained unbroken. Who first connected Roland's legendary sword stroke with the Brèche remains unknown. What actually happened at Roncevaux was that the rearguard was wiped out by a Basque ambush.

Normal Route. Ungraded. From the Brèche hut follow a trench in snow, rising in a curve R to the snow covered terminal moraine of the little glacier above. From this point the whole of the Brèche is first seen. The track rises over an easy snow slope to the gap itself, 2807m.

Go on to the S side and turn R on a path running W beneath the wall to an abrupt end 700m. ahead and a few m. from an isolated needle, the Doigt. The gap between the wall and the Doigt is known as the Fausse Brèche. Go through this gap to the N side (snow) and continue W up the gentle slope of the Taillon E ridge to the summit. 1¾ h. from hut. To the E, the Marboré, Cilindro and Monte Perdido form a fine group. The line of the Ordesa canyon can be seen to the S.

Brèche hut to Delgado/Goriz hut (2250m.)

This interesting high level route, passing along the top of the Gavarnie cirque, includes the greater part of the classic approach from Gavarnie to Monte Perdido and associated objectives. Note that a shorter, easier and altogether less interesting route from the Brèche runs at a much lower level over 2 saddles and across the head of the Ordesa valley to the Spanish hut site in 3½-4h. This route is the one marked prominently on maps. The other, described below, is not generally indicated.

Go up to the Brèche, as for the previous route, and turn L (E) on a path dropping beneath the S wall of the Casque. The path soon crosses a short but steep snow slope, close under the wall. A late spring snowfall here can produce avalanche conditions for some weeks, though rare. Continue ESE and rise under the wall to a crumbling sloping ledge with steel cable fastened along the wall above the Col des Isards (2749m.)

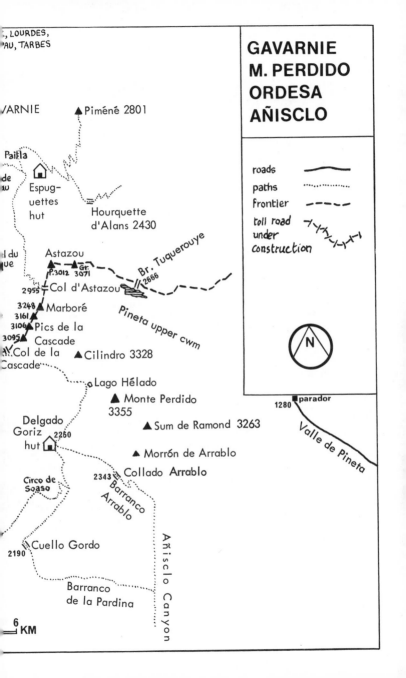

, LOURDES,
'AU, TARBES

GAVARNIE
M. PERDIDO
ORDESA
AÑISCLO

roads
paths
frontier
toll road
under
construction

N

VARNIE ▲ Piméné 2801

Pailla

de
lu Espug-
uettes
hut

Hourquette
d'Alans 2430

l du ▲ Astazou
que P.3012 ▲ Gr.
3071 Br. Tuquerouye
2666
2955 Col d'Astazou
3248 ▲ Marboré
3161 Pineta upper cwm
3106 ▲ Pics de la
3095 ▲ Cascade
N. Col de la ▲ Cilindro 3328
Cascade

o Lago Hélado

▲ Monte Perdido
3355

1280 ■ parador

Delgado
Goriz 2250 ▲ Sum de Ramond 3263
hut

Valle de Pineta

▲ Morrón de Arrablo

Circo de
Soaso 2343 Collado Arrablo
Barranco
Arrablo

Cuello Gordo
2190
Barranco
de la Pardina

Añisclo Canyon

6
KM

below on your R. The path then drops and at the end of the wall turns L and climbs into a broad open slope between the Casque and the Tour. Bear R and reach a broad terrace passing beneath the S slopes of the Tour. Follow along the terrace until a cairn is reached indicating the point to turn L to a short chimney up the low wall to the L, which is climbed to reach an upper terrace. This chimney may be half choked with snow but can be climbed by rocks on its L side. On the upper terrace , continue E then bear L to the edge of the upper wall of the Gavarnie cirque at a point a little under one km. E of the Tour.

Continue E along the top of the cirque to the Col de la Cascade (2931m.). Impressive view into the cirque; the massive head of the Cilindro is seen to the E. The path, marked by small cairns, continues E, rising a little above the 3000m. contour then curving SE to pass under the SW ridge of the Cilindro. At this point the NW face of Monte Perdido is first seen across a deep valley falling to the S. Turning the end of Cilindro SW ridge, the path drops into the head of this valley, down to a frozen tarn, Lago Hélado (Etang Glacé), SE of the Cilindro and NW of Monte Perdido.

From the tarn the path turns S down the valley over rock and snow on slopes L of a stream and moving gradually away from it. Lower down it reaches grass terraces separated by a series of low rock walls (cairns). The Delgado/Goriz hut is seen below. Reach it by taking the easiest way down the terraces. About $5\frac{1}{2}$h. from the Brèche hut.

LE CASQUE 3006m.

Normal Route. Ungraded. As for the previous route to where the path turns L into a broad open slope between the Casque and the Tour. Halfway up the slope turn L and reach a point a little to the S of the Casque summit by moderate slopes of boulders and snow patches. Turn R and scramble over rocks to the top. 2h. from Brèche hut.

LA TOUR (DU MARBORÉ) 3009m.

Normal Route. Ungraded. As for the previous route start, continued to where the path reaches the edge of the Gavarnie cirque. Turn W along the edge and rise by easy slopes to a point a little to S of the summit. Ascend R to top. 3h. from hut. La (sic) Tour, IGN mapping.

Casque - Tour. Grade, PD. From the Casque reverse the ascent route to where you leave the Delgado/Goriz route. Now turn N up the slope, then bear R (E) up a broad steep gully of boulders and snow to the top of the Tour. About 1h. from the Casque.

Note: The Tour N face has a classic rock climb graded ED- of about

250m. The main part of the route is on the upper wall of the cirque beneath the Tour, starting from the upper terrace; first climbed 1956 by J.Ravier and C.Dufourmantelle. The first winter ascent was made in January 1973 by R.Despiau, L.Audoubert and F.Tomas; they spent 4 nights on the face.

PIC DU MARBORÉ 3248m.

IGC 3253m. The highest of the peaks round the Gavarnie cirque.

Normal Route. Grade, F+. As for the Delgado hut route above, to a point midway between the Cascade col and the SW ridge of the Cilindro. Here turn L and climb easy slopes a little E of N, over rocks and snow, then bear NNW up the broad back of the mountain to its top. Diversion from track below, one km. plus. $3\frac{1}{2}$-4h. from Brèche hut.

Col d'Astazou 2951m.

Between the Marboré (S) and Petit Astazou (N). Grade, PD+. Note there are 2 ridge gaps, S = 2951 and N = 2955, separated by a rock spine crest, 2983m. While the true pass is S, you go through the N gap. The greater part of the route is a simple walk, but the upper sections involve a certain amount of serious scrambling.

From Gavarnie follow the Piméné path (above) to the Pailla pastures, to the second signpost marked "Plateau de Pailla Alt.1800". From here ignore all paths. Bear half R towards a small stream, cross it and rise to a little saddle (grass) with a small clump of pines to the L. Cross the saddle, turn R up the slope and find red and yellow marked stones in the turf; follow them SW. The line of stones soon develops into a clear path, followed almost horizontally above the woods for about 30 min. when it reaches the Rochers Blancs, a long white escarpment falling steeply down the slope beneath the W flanks of the Petit Astazou. The track over the Rochers Blancs, taken in a rising traverse, is clearly marked. Diversion from it may lead to difficulties. On leaving this part, the path continues S along the slope and soon reaches the W ridge of the Petit Astazou (brown rocks). This is crossed and the path runs to a torrent cascading down from the col through the broad gully between the Astazou and the Marboré. The climb proper starts here. Go up the escarpment over which the cascade falls, keeping well to the L under the Petit Astazou. At the top of the escarpment the path continues to rise steeply to a second then a third escarpment; it then bears half R, ascends rocks and turns L over slopes of snow or boulders to reach a final escarpment beneath the col. Reach a gully at the far L end of this escarpment, climb it, and at its head (blocked) turn R up over rock to reach a horizontal ledge. Move along it R, and at its end climb L, then bear

Mondarruego Wall, Ordesa Canyon.

half **L** diagonally across a steep slope to reach the col. 5h. from Gavarnie.

PICS D'ASTAZOU   Grand 3071m.   Petit 3012m.

Sp. Picos de Astazu: IGC (E) 3080m. (W) 3024m. These twin peaks are a prominent feature from Gavarnie. From the saddle between the 2 tops (Col Swan, 2964m.) falls a long, narrow and apparently very steep gully. This is Couloir Swan, first climbed in 1885 by Francis Swan and the guide Henri Passet. Swan was a friend of Russell, who thought Swan's exploit not a little foolhardy. While this great gully is not particularly difficult, conditions can vary considerably during the course of a season. The easiest route is from Col d'Astazou.

Normal Route. Grade, F+. From Col d'Astazou (above, PD+) turn N along the crest and on reaching the summit ridge turn R to gain the Petit Astazou in 20 min. from the col. Continue E along the ridge and drop a little on the N side to reach the head of the Swan couloir. Now the ridge E, keeping a little below crest on S side, then rise to the ridge and follow it to the Grand Pic. About 40 min. from the Petit. To the SE the view is spectacular. Across a high cirque surrounded by the Marboré, Cilindro and Perdido to the R, and a line of frontier peaks to the L, one looks down the long Pineta valley of which the cirque forms the head. Long ago it must have formed the upper basin of a great glacier, witnessed by moraines almost 40km. away and at a height of no more than 800m. above sea level.

ORDESA CANYON

Fr. Arazas valley, after the name of the principal stream. This is generally considered to be the most beautiful valley in the Pyrenees. Not a narrow gorge, the park-like lower valley is bordered by great ochre and saffron coloured cliffs of a uniform height; round the Circo de Salarons, an inlet to the N of the main valley, the more highly coloured walls are fantastically buttressed. At the Port de Gavarnie the new toll road on the Spanish side down to Torla gives the quickest access from France. The Ordesa entrance is about 3km. before Torla. From the Col du Pourtalet, the shortest road access is 60km. Pedestrian and other routes are as follows.

From Port de Gavarnie (Boucharo)
Cross the frontier by the road and follow a path branching L from it, WSW down a long open valley. The path, crossing the road twice, is obvious and needs no description. After 5km. cross the Ara river by a humpbacked stone bridge at the hamlet of San Nicolas de Bujaruelo (1338m.)

where the road is rejoined; customs post. Follow the road down the beautiful wooded Ara valley, through a gorge, to the Viejo/Navarros bridges junction (1070m.) at the Ordesa valley entrance above Torla (6km. from Bujaruelo, 3h. from Port de Gavarnie). Turn L up the bends of the road leading into the valley. The Parador (State hotel) stands above the road to the L. Continue to the roadhead, about 5km. from the Navarros bridge; carpark and café (1340m.). About $4\frac{1}{4}$ h. from Port de Gavarnie.

From Brèche hut by the Circo de Salarons

Grade, PD. Go up to the Brèche de Roland and down the cone of debris fallen from it on the S side. At the foot of the cone turn R and follow the 2780m. contour level as closely as possible in a curve WSW to reach the Collada Blanca (2822m.), a saddle N of the Pico Blanca (2923m.). Through this saddle, descend W in a long snow-filled gully. At its foot turn L (S) down a slope to a flat area – tarn bed – Llano de Salarons (2426m.). Cross this and drop down a rock terrace to a second similar basin, the Aguas Tuetas (2328m.). Pass along the L-hand (E) side of this and, after crossing a rock terrace at its S end, continue S until you arrive at the top of a short steep chimney in which iron pegs are fixed. Go down the chimney and bear half L to reach the top of a short rock pitch also with iron pegs. At the foot turn R and R again to the start of a path which runs horizontally in an anti-clockwise direction along a curving ledge high up on the majestically buttressed and highly coloured wall of the strange Circo de Salarons.

The path then descends the cliffs in broad sweeps, crosses a stream and follows down its L bank, though at some distance from it; the path continues across a parched area of rocks until it reaches thin woods (forestry biv. hut) through which it passes to meet the Ordesa valley road just under one km. from the carpark. $5\frac{1}{2}$ h. from Brèche hut.

From Brèche hut by the Circo de Cotatuero

Grade, PD. As for the previous route to below the debris cone. Continue straight down (S) over snow slopes then boulders and slabs on the R side of the Brecha torrent to reach a flat area (Llano, 2407m.). To the SE is the strange, flat, rounded dome of the Pico Descargador, pt. 2622m. You have now passed a fork L crossing the saddle N of this summit for the most direct way to the Delgado hut. Continue S, under W side of the dome by rock terraces, falling gradually until the path reaches the edge of the upper wall of the great Circo de Cotatuero near pt. 2338. Turn L (E) along the rim of the wall and drop by terraces to the head of a kind of upper valley falling to the SW. Follow L bank of the stream and cross it by wading at a point marked by cairns; strongish current and bed of small boulders. Follow down the R side to the

Tozal del Mallo, Ordesa Canyon.

rim of the wall of the Circo de Cotatuero proper, where the stream drops into the cirque in a magnificent fall (2018m.). Breathtaking view of the E wall of the cirque.

The path, very close to the top of the fall, turns R onto the face of the wall. Here a number of iron pegs, both for the feet and hands, have been fixed to facilitate the otherwise very difficult horizontal traverse of this wall section. The pegs were fixed by a Mr Burton, a keen stalker of the ibex, in the 1880s. They are still firm. At the end of the first section of the traverse descend on pegs for a few m. to the second horizontal traverse, which reaches a flat ledge and the head of a chimney. Go down it to a broad ledge, from where the path winds down over easy rocks and comes finally to the great pine woods on the western side of the cirque; forestry biv. hut. The path continues comfortably downwards until it arrives at the main track going up the Ordesa valley at a point rather under one km. beyond the roadhead carpark. 6 h. from the Brèche hut.

Ordesa Valley to Delgado/Goriz hut

The road from Torla (1033m.) proceeds N for 3 km., past a hotel and campsite, to the Navarros bridge (1070m.) at the Ordesa valley entrance, then climbs E by several bends to the State hotel. Above it rises the Mondarruego wall, which holds one of the most severe climbs opened on the N side of the canyon. The 4 Spanish climbers who achieved the first ascent in 1964 made 2 night bivouacs on the face of 400m. and spent 23 h. in actual climbing.

The road ends 3.5 km. further up the valley; large carpark, picnic site, café (1340m.). To the NW, standing out from the W corner of the Circo de Salarons, is the Tozal del Mallo (2263m.). This rock tower, rising from a forest pedestal, has an all but vertical S face of 400m. At first sight it gives the impression that a tower from the Dolomites has strayed into the Pyrenees. The face is riven by a number of vertical cracks from top to bottom. First climbed in 1957, several routes and variations have now been established on the face. All are graded TD or ED.

Eastwards from the end of the road a good path goes up the valley on the L side of the stream, at varying distances from it, through delightful woods and clearings; it soon passes across the entrance to Circo de Cotatuero to the N. Above the cliffs at the W corner of the cirque is Punta Galliñero, a surrealist rock tower. This too has a route graded ED opened by 2 Spaniards in 1961.

Continuing, the path starts to climb through woods to the upper valley. When you emerge from them, look back across the top of the woods for a view of the lower valley of great beauty. To the R of the path the stream falls through a narrow gorge, the Estrecho. A path of a few m. leads to the top of the fall. The gently rising pastures of the upper valley are ascended gradually L (NE). Here the walls of the valley appear less high, due to the increased height of the valley floor, and also less colourful. Keeping to the L side of the stream, the path reaches a stretch called Los Grados – the Steps – where the stream falls over a series of shallow terraces decorated by dwarf pines. So perfect is it that it appears to have been artificially built, but this is not so.

The path curves round into the austere head of the valley, the Circo de Soaso; ahead, first the Sum de Ramond, then the massive S flank of the Perdido come into sight. The path crosses the stream by a bridge then climbs SE on to an escarpment and returns NNW in a steady ascent above it. The old Goriz hut (2160m.) is seen ahead, the path rising to it over rock outcrops in the pasture. The Delgado hut (2250m.) lies some 150m. beyond. About 4h. from the roadhead.

MONTE PERDIDO 3355m.

Fr. Mont Perdu. Misprinted 3335 on IGN/RP map 1985 Ed. Together with the Cilindro and Ramond, collectively grouped in Spain as Las Tres Sorores (= hermanas = sisters). The third highest peak in the Pyrenees. It is massive but has no great rockfaces. The northern approach to the normal route (below) and the mixed N face route are described in the companion volume, Pyrenees Central.

Normal Route. Grade, F. From the Delgado/Goriz hut follow in reverse the route to this hut from the Brèche hut (see earlier), by going up the small track with cairns to the Lago Hélado (c.2985m.), between the Cilindro and Perdido; 2¼h. from Delgado hut, 4½h. from Brèche hut. At the tarn turn R (SE) and climb on snow on the L (N) side of a low ridge of rock falling from the visible summit of Perdido. Continue beside this subsidiary ridge, in a broad couloir, until the route bears round steeply to the L under a rockband and into a broad gully (snow). At the head of this, climb a short steep bar of boulders to the R and so reach snow slopes below the summit cone. Bear L and rise in a curve to the summit, reaching it from the N; about 1½h. from Hélado tarn.

Alternative descent to Delgado hut. Grade, F. From the summit descend S for 50m. over boulders, then turn L down rocks and boulders to arrive at the head of the Ramond glacier, lying between Perdido and the Sum de Ramond (3262m. IGC 3254m.). The snowy glacier is usually reached from the rocks without difficulty, but there may be a small bergschrund late in the season. Go down into the bowl at the head of the glacier then bear R (S) down its slope. All the ground hereabouts is badly shown on all maps. Well below the foot of the snow

Monte Perdido (L) and Cilindro (R) from the NW – Pineta cirque side.

slope is an isolated tower, the Morrón de Arrablo. When about 600m. from this tower, turn R and pass horizontally on very broad terraces beneath the southern slopes of Perdido. Taking a line a little N of W continue on the terraces, dropping gradually until the outward route is reached by a broad curving gully of boulders. From here descend the small track with cairns to hut below. Summit to hut, about $3\frac{1}{2}$h.

CILINDRO DE MARBORÉ   3328m.

Fr. Cylindre. IGN 25m.V 3325m. The most characteristic limestone profile in the district.

From Delgado/Goriz hut. Grade, PD. As for Perdido normal route to the Lago Hélado. From this tarn a long broad gully of boulders or snow is seen rising steeply to the W to a saddle on the broad SW ridge. Climb this gully and from the saddle climb one of the 2 short chimneys on the R to reach the crest of the SW ridge, rising in a gentle slope to the summit. 4h. from hut.

From Brèche hut. Grade, PD. Follow the route to the Delgado hut (see earlier), to a point E of the Col de la Cascade, before the track curves SE to pass under the foot of the Cilindro SW ridge. Turn NE then E to climb by a long, broad gully of boulders and snow to the ridge saddle reached by the approach from the Delgado hut in previous route. Continue as for latter to summit. $4\frac{1}{2}$-5h. from Brèche hut.

Note: There are 2 rock climbs of high quality on the Cilindro. One, opened in 1957 on the NE face, a vertical wall seen in profile from the Lago Hélado, is graded TD. The other, first climbed in 1964 on the equally vertical N face, seen from the Astazou, is graded TD+.

Marboré, Cilindro and Monte Perdido from the W. Head of the
Grande Cascade (lower L) falling into the Gavarnie cirque.

Añisclo Canyon

Maps: IGN/RP 50m. n.4. EA 40m. n.204. The Añisclo canyon, or Valle de Añisclo, is a deep narrow trench about 10 km. in length, running N-S, with its head about 3 km. SE of the Sum de Ramond. The most convenient point of departure for exploring this remarkable gorge is the Delgado/Goriz hut. However, the gorge can be entered at the bottom from a good small road now made from Escalona to the entrance at the San Urbano bridge.

The area was first explored in detail in the late 1870s by Franz Schrader, a well known explorer and cartographer of the Pyrenees. A Frenchman, in spite of his name, who named a large number of features in the valley and the surrounding area. These names have become established and are used in French guides to the region. Some confusion has resulted, since very few of Schrader's names are to be found on Spanish maps.

The canyon, through which the Rio Vellos flows, falls from 2200m. at its head to about 900m. at its S end where it joins the Rio Aso. The lower part is thickly wooded.

From Delgado hut by the Barranco de la Pardina.

From the hut take first the path leading SE down into the Ordesa valley but, instead of dropping into its head, follow another path which passes along the curving top of the Ordesa valley cliffs. In some 3 km. the Gordo saddle (2190m.) appears to the S. Cross this and follow a path SSE, which reaches the head of the Pardina barranco (ravine). This lies W-E and falls to join the Añisclo canyon at R-angles. The path first runs along the top of the cliffs on the N side of the ravine then turns steeply down into it. At the foot of the cliff the path follows above the N side of the torrent until it joins the path on the W side of the stream in the Añisclo canyon, at a point about halfway down its length. $3\frac{1}{2}$ h. from hut.

From Delgado hut by the Barranco Arrablo (Fon Blanca).

This route needs more care than the previous one. From the hut take a line ESE to reach the Collado Arrablo (2343m.), an obvious saddle between the southern slopes of the Sum de Ramond and the Sierra Custodia. Cross the saddle and bear SE down the head of a valley (pasture and rock terraces) keeping to the R, to reach the ridge flanking the Arrablo gorge, and running SE towards the Añisclo canyon. At first

Añisclo Canyon, SE wall.

sight no route down into the gorge seems possible. Follow along the edge of the gorge for about 500m. distance to c.2180m. Now turn L into the gorge down a steep slope of boulders; you will reach a ledge about 50m. below, which runs round the head of the gorge. On coming to it, turn L and follow it round, clockwise, to reach the opposite (NE) side of the gorge. After rising a little, the route drops obliquely down the steep side of the gorge by grass and rock terraces. The track leads down to the torrent then passes through thin woods to reach the canyon not far below its headslopes. About 3h. from hut. This route line is now correctly marked on the IGN/RP map, but remains wrong on the EA map (1983 Ed).

Note: A high level route on the N side of the Fon Blanca to enter the uppermost part of the main gorge at the so-called Añisclo col is more exposed, slightly tricky, with a couloir pitch possibly in steep frozen snow, and rock pitches of I+ with a section of III. However, it is a frequented route.

PINETA VALLEY

Included here as the Spanish approach to routes on the less frequented N side of Monte Perdido (Pyrenees Central). The valley, almost straight, extends WNW for 14km. from Bielsa (1053m.) to a roadhead at the Mte. Perdido Parador (hotel); campsite, café, inn (1280m.). At the back of the valley a 1000m. high headwall (Circo de Pineta) forms a huge concave bowl; a fairly good but small path climbs this to the Pineta upper cwm and a large tarn sporting no less than 4 names (2590m.) on the N side, under the Tuquerouye gap and hut (2666m.). Irregular but cairned tracks ascend S towards Monte Perdido. By this approach to bivouac in upper cwm (ruined stone huts), about 5h.

Appendix

MAPS

Since the previous edition of this guide entire series of maps have disappeared. Cuts in budgets and planning, and political rancour, have left the visitor with a less satisfactory and unsettled situation and future in the late 1980s. First to the Spanish side of the range.

In Spain, as before, government topographical mapping available to the public is old, out of date and quite difficult to find in local towns and villages. The military has a series of modern large scale maps designated 'military restricted' which is not sold to the public. Former series of French (IGN) mapping, including new issues since 1975 now withdrawn, extended some way S across the frontier, but in the last 5 years current IGN mapping has been cropped back so that only the minimum amount of Spanish terrain is shown consistent with meanderings in the frontier. This practice has been pursued to the ridiculous extremes of masking out 'excessive' display of the Spanish side with legends and tourist information.

The visitor is therefore confined to using the commercial EA series which now extends right across the Pyrenees West zone as described in this vol. The scale of these maps is not consistent and varies from 40m. to 25m. (while others are 50m.). Inevitably these maps are somewhat crude and have several major shortcomings. Although contoured, they rarely show areas of rock and cliff, and forest zones are mostly absent. In other matters of detail, eg. paths and the distinction between pistes (forest tracks) jeep roads, and small metalled roads, vague approximations in category and direction on the ground soon become evident. Many paths used in the course of walks and ascents are not shown. A plethora of missing detail can be cited but a number of improvements can be detected from 1985.

France: The government agency IGN produces topographical mapping across the French side of the range. In 25m. scale the former park maps (PNP) have been replaced by another 4 sheets in the IGN Violet series (273, 274, 275, 276), laid down in a somewhat different pattern. These maps are due to be withdrawn (though still available in 1987), and in any case were never planned to be extended as a series covering areas outside the PNP. In 1985 a completely new plan for 25m. scale tourist maps (17 in all) was issued, none of which has appeared to date. This plan includes horizontal and upright formats of differing sizes and there are gaps between them, so that the mapping is not continuous. 3 maps based on the normal 25m. grid pattern in double size sheets, known as Double Blue, were issued for the extreme E (Mediterranean) end of the range between 1978-81, which seem to contradict the series scheme now awaited.

National grid pattern sheets in the 25m. scale are small (4 cover the area of each 50m. scale map) and are now quite out of date. Previous reference to these maps in the guide is now expunged.

Going down in scale the next series in 50m. comes firstly in a national grid pattern which has been subjected to simplified sheet numbering and some modification to ground shown along the frontier. These maps were always cited in the guide and remain so. The quality of these maps is superior to the newer RP ones (see below) but their updating has declined in order, no doubt, to thrust the RP mapping upon the public. As with all standard pattern mapping, no overprinting of special information is given, but many purists will continue to prefer the clarity of this edition. Some sheets show more Spanish ground than any other mapping, eg. 1648 Gavarnie.

About 24 sheets in the 50m. grid pattern are needed to cover the Pyrenees along the French side. In the early 1980s IGN collaborated with the RP organization to introduce a new series of 50m. scale maps, of much larger format, to extend along the range end to end.

This project has recently been completed in a set of 11 maps (10 if the superfluous double depth n.9 above n.8 is discounted). The formats are quite irregular, being square, horizontal or upright willy-nilly. Overlapping of sheets occurs to an extent up to 50%. What appears to be the final pattern only emerged in July 1986. Prior to this there had been 3 changes in the pattern plan since inception, and in some sheet number areas 2 maps of different extent and format exist. The earliest editions did not have the Spanish ground masked but now (1986) it is mostly vigorously obliterated. A more serious retrograde step is a change in the tonal values of inks used to print major features, eg. forests, easting relief shading, etc. The result, with a massive amount of visitor information overprinted (often too large) on the maps, is that many areas are grey toned and difficult to read. This applies to miniscule lettering and figures in particular, and in the clarity of contours. The problem varies from sheet to sheet. Bearing in mind that the base for this mapping is the fine 50m. grid pattern series (see above), and the amount of criticism already generated by the RP series, IGN will doubtless endeavour to rectify the poor appearance of these maps. Notwithstanding these comments the editors have decided to base all references in this edition of the guide, in so far as France is concerned, on the IGN/RP series.

In smaller scale again, the IGN 100m. Green series of tourist maps cover the Pyrenees in 4 sheets (69, 70, 71, 72). Except for n.69, very little ground in Spain is shown, and there is some deliberate masking in the other sheets. This is fairly good mapping (but not as good as the 100m. grid pattern series, ignored in this guide) and useful for general planning. For motoring the IGN 250m. Red series covers the Pyrenees in 2 sheets (113, 114). The W sheet (113) shows a lot of Spanish ground, the other rather less so. Beware about the perplexities of changes in road numbers and classification in France; in this respect Michelin uncontoured but equally good road maps can be more up to date. In all the foregoing mapping some old road numbers are retained, others are revised to new numbering, whereas others have a mixture of the two.

In summary, from W to E, the relevant mapping for the Pyrenees West guide as now presented is as follows. All maps are obtainable from West Col Productions.

EA series:

40m.	227	Roncevalles-Roncal
40m.	201	Ansó-Hecho
25m.	202	Candanchú-Canfranc
25m.	203	Panticosa-Formigal
40m.	204	Valle de Ordesa – Vignemale

IGN 25m. Violet series:

273	Aspe-Ossau	275 Gavarnie-Néouvielle
274	Balaitous-Vignemale	276 Néouvielle-Vallée d'Aure

IGN 50m. grid pattern series:

1447	Larrau	1647	Argelès-Gazost	1747	Campan
1547	Laruns-Somport	1648	Gavarnie	1748	Vielle-Aure

IGN/RP 50m. series:

2 Pays Basque Est   3 Béarn   4 Bigorre

IGN 100m. Green series:

69 Pau-Bayonne   70 Pau-Bagnères de Luchon

IGN 250m. Red series: 113 Pyrénées Occidentales

FOREIGN TECHNICAL PUBLICATIONS

Some 150 volumes in French, Spanish and Catalan have been issued in the last 15 years, for walking, trekking, touring, backpacking and climbing, inclusive of catalogue type publications (hut lists/accommodation, etc.). These are constantly changing, disappearing or coming up again in other forms.

In France the Ollivier series deals with serious technical climbs in about 12 vols – issued in French, Spanish or Catalan according to the area. In Spain numerous independent technical climbing guides are published in the native languages, notably the CEC series.

The Pyrenees High Level Route (HRP) is covered in one volume and is available in French, Catalan and English. The GR 10 low level way along the French side of the range comes in 5 vols – in French only. There is a five-fold duplication in French guides for walkers over some areas of the Pyrenees. New GR touring routes and circular excursions are constantly being introduced by government and local agencies on the French side, which merely aggravates and confuses the multiplicity of choice.

Index